FINDING MY TRIBE

A Journey in Finding Life Calling

Advantage
BOOKS

Marti ANDERSON

Published by: ADVANTAGE BOOKS™
Longwood, Florida, USA
www.advbookstore.com

In this memoir some names have been changed.

Library of Congress Catalog Number: 2015950224

Many interior photos by Dr. Gordon Larson
Author Photo by Sarah Gnadig
Cover Design: KeithLocke.com

First Printing: September 2015
15 16 17 18 19 20 21   10 9 8 7 6 5 4 3 2 1
Printed in the United States of America

For Larry…

who has journeyed with me in love

Marti Anderson

THANKS TO...

Dad (and Mom in Heaven) for being my heroes.

Nick and Jared for believing in their mom.

Romaine in forbearance with her older sister, and help with pictures!

Scott Tompkins for wisdom in editing.

Janice Rogers for persistence in training apprentice writers.

Janet Benge who inspired me to dream big.

Marti Anderson

Table of Contents

Marti Anderson

Marti Anderson

PROLOGUE

THE UPWARD CALL

I was just a small child, picnicking with my family on a fine summer day in Kentucky, when I watched a young man with fascinated interest. He was inching slowly up the face of a sheer cliff. A hand grasped higher... a foot lifted, rested on an outcropping of gray stone. I was mesmerized by the seeming impossibility of his ascent. Was it real? He was hanging onto a rough perpendicular wall, and my young mind did not know this was possible. It was 1949, my parents later told me, and I was less than two years old.

This vivid memory became a kind of metaphor for my life and family. My parents were always climbing as they pressed forward in their callings. And all of us are called to higher ground. God sometimes challenges us to take risks that are more impossible than climbing that cliff at High Bridge Park.

The Apostle Paul writes in Philippians 3:13-14 (NIV): Brothers, I do not consider myself yet to have taken hold of it. But one thing I do: Forgetting what is behind and straining toward what is ahead, I press on toward the goal to win the prize for which God has called me heavenward in Christ Jesus.

My parents – Gordon and Mildred "Peggy" Larson – were always pressing toward that upward call. For 38 years they served with the Christian and Missionary Alliance in the jungles of Dutch New Guinea (Irian Jaya, now Papua, Indonesia). They could have been successful in other careers. Dad was a gifted musician who played regularly with the U.S. Army Band at the Capitol in Washington DC. As a young woman Mom worked in a civil service job at the Pentagon. But God spoke to each of them about a different calling – taking the gospel to Stone Age tribes in the southwest Pacific.

The two met at the Washington Bible Institute, and a few months later Gordon proposed to the stylish beauty with the honey colored hair. After an elegant wedding in Washington D.C. in August, 1946, they began attending Nyack Bible College in New York to prepare for their upward climb as missionaries.

When I consider the sacrifices it took for them to pursue their missions calling – spiritually, mentally, even physically – I'm still amazed. What made them want to achieve so much? Why were they such spiritual mountain climbers?

Mom and Dad learned three languages. Dad formed orthographies, dictionaries for Moni and Dani languages, and finally translated books of the New Testament into Western Dani. Both became conversant in Indonesian, the trade language. And Mom taught the Danis to read, producing primers to teach vowels, consonants, short words. When a Dani mastered all of the primers and could read sentences, he or she would receive the book of Mark…and later a whole New Testament.

Having parents like these inspired me to reach higher than I would have dreamed, and to trust God in impossible situations. I've followed my own upward call now for 60 years and it's taken me to places like Malaysia, India, Egypt, Europe, and the Central Pacific. And I am still climbing.

Life stories—callings—are composed of the beads of days strung into years that pass imperceptibly into decades. Or to change the picture…the series of rocky cliffs climbed merge into mountain ranges of accomplishment. And when one stands on a summit toward the end of life gazing over the terrain, they may be stupefied, bewildered--like my parents--that God could accomplish so much through them.

I hope you recognize God also has a call on your life. Each calling is so diverse… there are many ways to find your tribe, and each upward journey requires faith and endurance. As you read these stories watch how unexpected life lessons propel us forward into the exciting journey He's prepared.

NURTURING THE CALL

PASSAGES

One of the most difficult parts of being a missionary kid is the leaving. It was not a "see you later" kind of leaving. It could be months or years until we saw our loved ones again. Our first taste of these painful goodbyes happened just before we left on the ship for New Guinea.

Mom and Dad needed to attend Wycliffe's Summer Institute of Linguistics (SIL) in Oklahoma to prepare for their work with the Christian and Missionary Alliance. We were unaware of their plan to leave my sister Romaine and me with each set of grandparents for six weeks.

One morning I awoke to find Mom and Dad gone.

"Where are they? When will Mom and Dad come back?" Grandma and Grandpa Larson reassured us they would return and their square frame house on Newland Ave. in Jamestown, New York was a treasure to explore. Painted light green outside, inside it was dark paneled and spacious, with a bright white kitchen. The stairs had two swinging doors entrances, and I found a great place to hide at the base of the stairs. The big dining room table had a green glass lamp above it with swinging tassels, and the shining glow made dinners personal, special. If I climbed to the high unfinished attic, there were treasures of old toys my father and Uncle Duane had owned, and boxes of old fashioned clothes. Romaine and I could spend hours exploring the musty wooden beamed attic.

Grandpa's grocery store was right across the street. Never having had a daughter, Grandma doted on us. I realize now she knew there would be a five year gap after we left for the mission field. We were now 3 and 5 years old, but when we next returned to the States we would be 7 and 9. She didn't complain.

I didn't know it then, but she'd had several miscarriages before giving birth to my dad. Back then she and Grandpa had prayed, "Oh Lord, if you let this next child live, we will give him like Samuel to your service. " So now she was keeping her word to God, offering her firstborn son for missions. She knew that once we left it would take one to two months to get an answer to an airmail letter. Telephone calls would be expensive if not impossible.

One bright morning she settled Ro and me on the front screened porch, and served us buttered homemade rye bread with milk coffee. I was entranced. It was warm and delicious. "Thank you, Grandma! Can I have more?" She gave refills over and over without complaint, between her energetic housecleaning.

After dinner we sat on the red tufted couch for evening devotions and felt warm and cherished. Then we were tucked into bed—the very beds our dad and Uncle Dewey had slept in! Cars rolled down the street outside and made whooshes, their lights rolling over the ceiling. Over and over, till I fell asleep.

After six weeks we took a long road trip in Grandpas's green DeSota. We were to be turned over to Grandma and Grandpa Bowman, Mom's parents, for the last six weeks. Ignorant of this I screamed and howled, after being kissed goodbye. "Why are they leaving us!" Sobbing, I looked out the backseat of the car at them growing smaller in the distance as we pulled away.

During the weeks at the Bowman's white frame farmhouse in Kentucky we were mostly cared for by Aunt Christine and Aunt Sue, Mom's younger sisters. Grandma Bowman was brisk and busy— cooking, cleaning, canning. We slept upstairs in the dormer bedroom where Mom used to sleep as a teenager. I loved that house too. On the wide front porch hung two swings where Romaine and I could rock back and forth, listening to the locusts sing in the summer heat.

Across from the wooden stairs in the living room was a coal stove where we gathered at night before bed, and Grandpa Bowman read the Bible. Sometimes he would say verses by heart—ones he had memorized years before. After Sunday church—a country church, where the men and women sat on opposite sides, facing each other—all the relatives gathered for a big fried chicken dinner. Aunt Inez and Uncle Evans and their families always joined us.

After a few weeks Ro and I moved to Aunt Inez's house where cousins Doris, Brenda, Billy, and Martha lived. During those weeks I was being infused with the Bowman values. Weeks of slow country life with rhythms of work, sleep, play among the kinsmen gave me understanding into my mother's life. The Bowman clan were also paying a price to send us to the Far East. Their prayers, giving, and ample packages helped sustain us those four years.

In September Mom and Dad arrived in Kentucky to rejoin us. Romaine and I were now part of the Bowman family. Our nuclear family was blurred into local tribal life. Every family gathering included aunts and uncles, cousins, and aging grandparents. But all that was going to change.

Mom and Dad were ordering supplies and packing drums to last us four years. Books and clothes, tools, kitchen utensils, medicine. That fall we hugged out Kentucky relatives goodbye, and headed back to Jamestown, New York where the drums would be packed and shipped to Dutch New Guinea.

Snowflakes fell softly and melted on the sidewalks of New York City. I lifted my face to the delicate wetness and sucked in the sharp cold. Hearing "I Saw Momma Kissing Santa Claus" wafting through an open doorway, I shivered with delight. Almost Christmastime! Bright lights twinkled through windows, cars rushed honking, Salvation Army bells ding-a-linged on corners.

I was five years old, excited to be in the big city shopping with my parents. In just a few days we'd be leaving on a Dutch freighter to cross the ocean, and I loved the fuss and exhilaration of change.

We said goodbye to Grandma at the square green house in Jamestown. She wouldn't be going to the docks in New York City, but would oversee the grocery store. This farewell was costly to her. She stood in the rich paneled living room and held onto Dad weeping silently. "Oh Gordon, "This is what we gave you to the Lord for. He's called you and Peggy to this." Her shoulders shook, as Dad held her and patted her back. Mom was crying too, wiping her eyes. Romaine and I looked on soberly. Maybe Grandma wondered if she'd see us again. Four years was a long time.

When we waved goodbye to Grandpa, Uncle Dewey, Aunt Petey, and our cousins at the docks in New York the leaving was more real to me. The loved ones looked smaller and smaller as we pulled away. Our cousins would be so grown up when we next saw them.

Mom said it would take two months to get to Dutch New Guinea. Romaine and I shared a stateroom, my parents another. There were beds on each side of our small room, with space for suitcases under them. No pictures, but small portholes gave light. Since our space was limited but time was not, Mom decided to begin my first grade home schooling in the Calvert Course. I memorized the alphabet and formed words slowly, as the ship pitched and rolled over rough seas. The sofa in the public living room slid back and forth in its alcove. "Cat, dog"…the couch slid and knocked to the right. "Hat, cap"….slip, knock to the left. After lunch Romaine and I wobbled behind Mom back to our bedroom, holding onto hand rails. Afternoon naps sometimes quieted our seasick stomachs.

The Dutch chef and chief steward celebrated Mom and Dad's birthdays on January 3rd and 15th with fluffy cake and flat, buttery frosting. Their attentiveness made up for the lack of sweetness. It took about a week to cross the Atlantic, and as the ship rolled through 40 foot high waves Mom got worried. "This isn't unusual weather for January," the ship steward assured Mom.

We viewed the white cliffs of England from a distance, later glided between massive gray rocks at the Straits of Gibraltar between Europe and North Africa. Time rolled by. We chugged slowly through blue water that Dad informed me was the Red Sea. Mom painted on deck, her water colors washing deep blue onto the white canvas.

Docking off the port of Jedda, Arabia where minarets poked sharply into the cobalt sky, I began to feel sick. I kept throwing up, had diarrhea, felt very hot. I could see my parents' worried faces, hear their concern. One evening Mom and Dad were up much of the night. It was hot in the tiny bedroom, and the air was foul from my vomit. Mom had changed my nightgown, washed my face with a cool cloth. Dad walked in. "How are you, Marlene?" he asked, taking my hand.

"Her temperature's 104, I don't think the antibiotic the ship's officer gave her has kicked in yet," Mom murmured. "I want to give her aspirin, but I think she'd throw it up." Mom stroked my blond hair. "I'm so concerned, Gordon. She's little, and here we are, anchored off Saudi Arabia. Surely God didn't send us out to allow us to lose a child. We haven't even reached New Guinea yet."

I heard Dad fervently praying over me as Romaine slept nearby in her bunk. "Lord, Marlene is yours. We are doing your work. Please heal her...have mercy upon us. Give Peggy and me your faith." Their voices droned on and I fell asleep.

Next morning when I awoke Dad was carrying in some ginger ale. "Hi, Honey. Are you feeling better?"

"I am, Daddy."

"Her temperature's down to 102--thank the Lord!" Mom exclaimed.

"Wonderful. God's answering prayer. Here's some more liquids. You'll like this, Marlene."

I took a sip. Tangy and delicious.

"I just came from the deck," Dad told Mom. They're unloading wheat--big sacks of it on the backs of dockworkers. No cranes. Amazing."

That night Dad took more time in devotions, thanking God fervently for my healing.

I slowly recuperated and eventually sat on deck, covered with a light blanket. Romaine and I colored, drew pictures. My younger sister was blond and so cute, I thought. She was quiet, but liked to joke. Since I was five and she was three she usually followed what I did. We made a good play team, though maybe I was too bossy sometimes.

Day after day the blue sky met the deep blue sea as we pressed forward through miles of waves. Dad got out his map and showed me how we had passed the south tip of Sri Lanka, crossed the Bay of Bengal, and chugged down through the Straits of Malacca to Singapore. There we packed up and debarked, after thanking the kind ship officers and shaking their hands. We then visited with mission workers in Singapore, and flew on to Bangkok.

Hot, exotic Bangkok. I watched the streets in amazement. Wiry dark haired men hurried by, carrying baskets of vegetables on poles slung over their shoulders. Men on bicycles pedaled heavily, pulling placid passengers behind them. What a strange, interesting land. As we strolled by an open restaurant door, I glimpsed a man eating noodles with chopsticks, sucking them up. Spicy smells….dripping sweat. We walked into a big temple and I gasped over the massive Sleeping Buddha. "What is that big statue, Daddy? He's lying down!"

"The Thai people worship this Buddha," Dad answered. "He is their god."

I marveled that people would think that a big carved stone could help them.

We lodged at the CMA guest house—an old colonial mansion with broad verandahs and thick white pillars. Sipping tea with my parents on the wide porch in the late afternoon, I rose to wander and chat. Coming back, I saw that the family's dog had lapped up my tea. "May I have another cup?" I asked the matron.

"No," she replied firmly. "You should have watched your cup!" I was surprised by her coldness. Grandma Larson had given me milk coffee over and over.

At night Mom and Dad tucked Romaine and me in bed beneath mosquito netting. I loved the gauzy tent and snuggled down to sleep. We were adventurers in strange lands, but safe with Mom and Dad, I realized. My five year old life was exhilarating, and I loved it.

JUNGLE TREK HOME

The move from America to Dutch New Guinea must have been difficult for my parents, but they didn't complain. They had prayed and prepared for years and were finally entering their life calling. I adjusted to each new place with calm, lively interest.

We flew to Manila, then to Biak, a tiny island on the equator, off the north coast of New Guinea. The hotel room in Biak was rustic, with whirring fans and gray sheets. Mom asked for fresh linens, but the ones the maid brought were just as dirty looking. The next morning the hotel lobby gleamed clean and spacious though, and we lavished Dutch chocolate sprinkles on our breakfast toast. Later, walking on the front lawn we met a man who held a snow-white cockatoo with a lemon-colored head plume. The bird cawed and talked to us, and Romaine and I were enchanted.

Our next flight took us by seaplane over cloud-covered mountains into New Guinea's interior. Never having landed on water, I was excited as we splashed onto Lake Paniai. A motorboat picked us up and chugged to a long pier where Lloyd and Dorie Van Stone greeted us, mid crowds of dark Ekari people. They sang tribal songs as we marched up the hill to a large log house where Mom said we would live for a few weeks. CMA missionaries Einar Mickelson and Walter Post had pioneered this station years ago, and now the Dutch government had an outpost also. Dad said we'd have to wait here until our supplies arrived—those drums containing clothes, bedding, dishes, and books that would last us for four years.

We waited over two months for those drums to arrive. Mom and Dad began to learn the Malay trade language and Dad occasionally took treks with Mr. Mickelson to other outposts. Romaine and I played with the lively Van Stone children, and began learning Malay as we hung out with Indonesian kids.

Finally the outfit arrived, was packed in metal containers (blicks), and we began the long trek to our new home…appropriately named Homejo. The three day journey by motorboat and hiking took five days. Mom became ill…the natives were starting to build a stretcher for her as she laid on the ground, but she finally sat up and pressed doggedly on. Romaine and I were carried on the shoulders of the Ekari—others carried the blicks. On and on our small caravan stretched, plodding slowly through muddy marshes, up rocky streambeds, and over the peaks of steep mountains.

The jungle was thick with undergrowth and hanging vines. I was glad to be carried, even though the carrier's sweat reeked as I jounced on and on. One day it rained all day, the trail turned to mud, and our progress slowed to a crawl. Rain pattered on the woven palm-leaf mat that was protecting me and my sturdy tribesman. When camp was finally set up for the night smoky food aromas wafted up from the campfire where rice boiled, and corned beef heated. Mom dished up the food onto tin plates, and we wolfed it down. "This is so good," I exclaimed.

"I'm glad you like it," Mom replied. "We're all so hungry I think we could eat most anything."

We slept cozily with Mom and Dad in sleeping bags in a small tent. The carriers were curled up by fires under thatched roofs they had made.

"How do they keep warm with no clothes like ours, Dad? They only have gourds and their head nets."

"I guess they're used to it, Marlene. And they all keep close to the fire," Dad replied.

By the end of the fifth day we reached the Kemandoga Valley where Homejo outpost perched on the hillside, with a roaring river far below. CMA missionaries Bill and Gracie Cutts ran down the hill to greet us.

"Welcome to Homejo," Bill said, with outstretched hand.

"Yes, we've been expecting you for several days," said Gracie. She gave us hugs. She was a chubby woman with a curly brown hair and a warm personality. "Come and have some tea. I have dinner cooking."

Our family settled into a small tin-roofed two storied frame house down the hill from the Cutts. After unpacking, Mom and Dad immersed themselves in language study with Moni helpers, Bill Cutts overseeing their progress.

Romaine and I ventured out the next day and were greeted by curious Moni children. We didn't speak each other's language, but managed to communicate with hand signs and smiles. I would point at an object, and a girl named Boma Kumba gave me the Moni name for it. She became my friend, even though she was perhaps three years older than me. Taller, with dark brown skin and short frizzy hair, she introduced me to a Moni child's life. She worked in the potato gardens to help her mother, so she couldn't always play with Romaine and me. And I noticed that her stomach stuck out, like all the other Moni kids. Dad explained that Moni kids had to eat lots of sweet potatoes and greens to get enough protein. They didn't have meat in their diet very often. Also, most of them probably had intestinal worms.

After a few weeks of playing with Boma Kumba and her friends we not only knew the names of things, but began putting small sentences together. Romaine and I burrowed through tall grasses in the field below our house, making tunnels and catching grasshoppers. We laughed, enjoying our hidden, green-stalked world. Later Boma Kumba showed us how to string the grasshoppers on tall stems and after roasting them crispy on the woodstove, eat them.

On Saturdays sometimes we visited villages with Aunt Gracie, inviting the Monis to Sunday services. Often rain torrents soaked the trail…we arrived home cold and muddy, eager for a hot supper and sudsy bath in the metal washtub. Life in this place wasn't easy, but it was adventurous and fun.

WICKET GATE

In my home school lessons I'd read about pioneers who came out West in covered wagons to live among the Indians. Our family now was living like those pioneers with woodstove, clothes washboard, kerosene lamps, and outhouse. Mom and Dad also were learning a language word by word, fitting nouns and verbs into sentences. We all were learning the culture of this primitive tribe who killed pigs to appease evil spirits, who plastered mud on their bodies and cut off finger joints when mourning the dead. We were planted among a tribe who owned their wives—one or more of them—and beat them if they disobeyed.

One time Aunt Gracie attempted to protect a woman whose husband was trying to shoot her in the leg with an arrow. Aunt Gracie got in the way and the arrow went into her own leg!

"Why would that man want to shoot his wife, Dad?" I questioned. We were sitting on the rattan couch in the living room, after supper.

"Well, the man bought his wife from her parents, so he believes he owns her. She made him very angry doing something, so he decided to teach her a lesson. He didn't want to kill her though, because she's valuable. She works his gardens, and gives him children"

"So the woman is safe, but now Aunt Gracie's leg has to heal?" I asked.

"That's right. The man is seeing that someone else was willing to suffer for his wife, and take her punishment. Maybe he will listen to what Uncle Bill is teaching about the Gospel."

I snuggled up to Dad as he read the Bible story for the night. We prayed for Aunt Gracie's leg to heal and the Moni woman and her husband to come to Jesus. And for Boma Kumba, my friend, and the grandparents back home in the States.

As Mom later tucked me into bed, I had a question. "Why can't I go barefoot like the other kids do? And can Romaine and I go frog hunting with our friends in the moonlight tomorrow, in the wet ditches?"

"You have to wear shoes because pig manure is on the paths, and tiny worms might burrow into any sore on your foot. And yes, tomorrow night you may go with Boma Kumba and her friends, down in the little valley close to the house. Remember, it's Friday night, so afterwards we'll have popcorn, and Dad will play his clarinet."

I was satisfied. "And you play the ukulele with Dad, and we'll all sing together."

One bright morning after an oatmeal breakfast and prayer Mom and Dad thoughtfully asked me if I would like to ask Jesus into my heart. I paused and considered what this meant. Jesus had died on the cross for me. I had seen pictures of Him knocking on a door...I knew we were to let Him come in.

I finally answered, "I want to do it by myself."

"That's alright," Dad said.

Later in the day I wandered down the grassy hill to the tin roofed, open-sided church. Two lines of roughhewn planks formed pews, with an aisle down the middle. I knelt on the hard packed dirt toward the front of the church, and leaned on the pew in front of me. "Oh God," I prayed. "Please come into my heart. Wash me clean. I want to be yours, Jesus."

I waited. Tall grasses near the church rustled in the breeze, puffy clouds drifted slowly in the pale blue sky. I didn't know what more to say. Finally I closed the prayer. "Thank you, God. I am yours."

Slowly I stood and trudged up the worn path to our house. A low wooden fence enclosed our yard to keep chickens and goats out. I opened the wicket gate and walked through—and the thought suddenly came, "Now I'm a Christian!"

During supper that night I told Mom and Dad what had happened. "I asked Jesus to come into my heart today."

"We're so happy for you, Marlene. You're in the Kingdom of God, with all of us," Mom said, hugging me.

Years later I read Little Pilgrim's Progress where Christian walked through the wicket gate on his way to the Celestial City, and his burden of sin fell off. My breath caught. The Holy Spirit had used our own front gate to remind me of my new-birth experience. How personal God is to each of us.

RATTAN BRIDGE

One afternoon I entered the back door and was surprised to see a Moni girl sitting on the wood floor in the corner of our kitchen. She looked to be a teenager, with the usual string skirt and a net hanging down her back, but she was cowering. Her eyes were large and frightened in her dark face.

"Amakane," I greeted her. She didn't answer.

"Mom, why is this girl here? I asked in English.

"Zigumina's hiding with us," Mom explained. "We're keeping her safe here because her relatives want to kill her."

"We are your friends," I told her in Moni. "Don't be afraid."

I found out later she was accused of "incest" immorality, and in this tribe that was punishable by death. She was blamed with sleeping with a man from another clan of the same moiety. Monis were strict about what part of the tribe a man could marry into. Accusers would break the legs of the suspected woman and throw her into the rushing river at the base of the valley. Somehow, the man would not be held so accountable—maybe because women were owned, but men weren't.

I was horrified and sad for Zigumina.. She looked so small and afraid in the corner of the kitchen, across from the wood stove. She wore a few beads around her neck, and her woven net hung down her back with almost nothing in it. That's all she had in the world. Could we really hide her for long? "Take care of her, Jesus," I prayed.

Later in the afternoon angry men came looking for Zigumina, and Mom barred the door. They shouted. "You can't have her," Mom cried back. She showed she meant business by throwing hot water through the slats of the rattan door. "You should treat your women kindly!" Finally the clansmen left, and after a good supper we gave Zigumina blankets and all went to bed.

But in the morning the young girl was gone—she had fled in fear. And word reached us later that the clansmen had caught her, indeed broken her legs, and thrown her into the rushing Kemandoga River.

Mom cried, "Oh Lord, take care of this poor girl. Save her life. Save her soul."

I was sad. It seemed unreal to me. Here I was, safe and protected by loving parents and a good Heavenly Father. Life was cruel and precarious for the Monis. That was why we had come to reach them with the Good News.

Uncle Bill and Aunt Gracie Cutts left for a year of furlough in the States, where they would spend time with relatives and tell churches about the mission work. Two ladies, Leona St. John and Rosalie Fenton arrived over the trail with a score of carriers and settled into a wooden frame house uphill from us. Aunt Leona was going to teach Monis how to read, and Aunt Rosalie as a nurse, would hold a clinic. When she opened up shop, I observed as she dispensed pills, gave injections, and bound up open wounds. Being conversational in Moni, I could occasionally interpret for her, give directions for how one should take the medicine. A nurse did so much good!

Before their arrival my parents had held clinic in the front yard. Eye ointment to those with yellow eye drainage, bandages to open wounds. They gave a series of penicillin injections to those who had yaws (frambosia), a horrible tropical disease that ate facial skin away. After the shots patients remained scarred, but disease free. And occasionally my dad even pulled teeth, when there was no other remedy.

Natives continued to gather on Sundays beneath the tin roofed, open-sided church. And there began to be more interest when a young Moni preacher arrived back from Enarotali to teach. His sermons were clear and effective—not as stilted as when the white man preached.

Some months later our family and Aunt Leona trekked down our Kemandoga Valley to scout out the land among a different tribe--the Wolani. I was seven years old now, and could mostly walk the trail, but while crossing the raging river deep in the valley, Dad insisted that Romaine and I were carried on the shoulders of Monis.

I still remember my father instructing the carrier to be extremely careful, and telling me to sit very still while we crossed the swinging rattan bridge. Looking down, I could understand why. Torrents of foaming green water crashed over large boulders, roaring downhill. If anyone fell in, there would be almost no way to rescue them.

After all crossed safely, our band trudged hours down valley and uphill to Kibigilagi, a large Wolani-Moni village of thatched houses. We pitched tents near the edge of a large village. I chatted with Aunt Leona and observed with interest that she was having a can of spaghetti heated for supper. What was Mom cooking? Dad conferred with Wolani chiefs and interpreters, and Romaine and I played.

The next day there was a large pig feast. Porkers squealed as they were shot in the heart with an arrow…men shouted…women carried greens, sweet potatoes, and taro root for a late dinner feast. Children ran and played, some of them blowing up pig bladders like small balloons.

Romaine and I watched. I had never seen anything like this! Native men were carving a score of carcasses, women were carrying cuts of pork to be cooked or given as gifts. Everyone was happy—they did not often get to eat meat, except for birds, frogs, or mice caught. They were all rejoicing together. And there would be not only the exchange of pork to solidify clan relationships, but also the celebration of several marriages, wives now formally given and paid for.

Later each evening we gathered with the tribe at an ugwai dance house built especially for the occasion by the leading chief. The sides and thatched roof were typical, but this floor was crisscrossed with pliant poles that made it bouncy. Wolanis and Monis joined in songs, unified refrains that they shouted as they jounced counter-clockwise in the house. Round and round we went, all of us singing. Happy, laughing….until it was time for Romaine and I to curl up in our sleeping bags.

On the afternoon of the last day the festivities were disrupted by cries of a young woman. We all watched as relatives dragged her down the trail, and she twisted her arms and shouted protests. "She doesn't want to marry an older man who has paid dowry for her," a Moni explained to me. "She likes another younger man." I watched as the girl's parents interceded on her behalf…and other clansmen argued that the older man had husband rights. The clansmen prevailed, and the girl was forced down the trail, wailing loudly.

On the trek home I wondered sadly about the young girl. Life could be so rich and yet so hard here. We carefully crossed the swinging rattan bridge, my parents praying. Old rattan could crack and break, and this was not a new bridge. Wolani and Moni life was full of danger and risk. Their lives were joyful but perilous.

And my parents were risking much to take the Gospel to them.

THE CALL

January of 1956 when I was eight years old we trekked back to Enarotali and flew to Melbourne, Australia, landing at my special island of Biak to change planes. Once every term the CMA paid for their missionaries to have a month long vacation in "civilization." It wasn't a real vacation for Dad, though. He was going to help teach a class in linguistics.

Romaine and I were awed by the big city, the traffic, and the crowds of people. "Look, there's a gas station!" Six year old Ro squealed. She only remembered seeing them in books. I was struck by the smell of gasoline and oil. And a strange, clean smell. It smelled like America, I decided.

We settled into a guesthouse for mission workers that included meals. Ro and I had our own room with bunk beds. We stayed there several days, and in the middle of the second night, something woke me. I felt a Presence with me—and it wasn't my sister. A voice spoke.

"I want you to be a missionary nurse,"

I considered, full of wonder. It must be the Lord. He was waking me like He did Samuel, and giving instructions. I sat up. The Presence was kindly, strong. And the words were clear.

"Yes, Lord," I answered Him. "I will do that." And He reminded of the Wolani tribe who were then unreached.

Lying back down I thought of dispensing medicine like Aunt Rosalie. She helped sick and hurting people get well. I liked the idea of practically helping people. There were so many people in Dutch New Guinea who needed medical care, tribes who had never even heard the Gospel.

So this is what it means to be commissioned...my call was specific. And I drifted back to sleep.

Later I told Mom and Dad how God had spoken to me, like Samuel. I was going to be a missionary nurse. They were glad and hugged me. "God will use you, Honey," Mom said.

Back home weeks later we settled into quiet family life among the Monis. Dad built Romaine and me a two roomed playhouse, each room with a kitchen shelf. We begged Mom for cucumbers and carrots to cut and munch in our "home." The Cutts had come back from furlough with a newly adopted son—Johnny, who was lively and articulate. We included him in our make-believe times.

That next Christmas, I was given an unusual present—I received it with wonder and delight. It was newly made, because the silver paint was still tacky wet. Made by Santa—by Dad? It was wooden nurse's kit filled with syringes, cotton balls, bandages. I was entranced. My own nurse's box! Beginning tools to help others.

And Romaine got her own little gas station, with metal cars. God was so good!

THE UPRISING

Once a year all of the mission workers gathered at Enarotali for "conference." For the adults this meant long hours of reporting, planning and prayer. For us children it meant hours of playing together outside-- speaking English rather than Moni or Ekari. The best times were meals shared with friends, and a fun night at the end where many gave hilarious skits or songs.

At one conference it was decided that my dad and fellow CMA worker Don Gibbons would trek ten days further east from Enarotali to establish a base among the Western Dani and Damal tribes. Two attempts to reach the valley had failed…but they would try again. Dad said they planned to build an airstrip so our two families could live there. We would move to Enarotali, as the men might be gone several months.

Dad trekked back to Homejo, packed up our belongings, and headed back over the trail to Enarotali, with carriers bearing the heavy metal blick containers. I loved the small log cabin we settled into. It had two tiny bedrooms upstairs, and was right next to the large log house that the older missionary Mickelson had built. We unpacked our clothes, dishes, and books and Mom hung curtains.

In June of 1956, before Dad left, a new baby brother was born in that log home, with a Dutch doctor attending. Danny was blond, red-faced, and Romaine and I jostled for turns to carry and burp him.

When the day came for Dad and Uncle Don to leave, Ro and I hugged Dad closely. It was early morning, and we were still in our pajamas.

"I need to go now, and I want you girls to be a big help to Mom while I'm away."

"Yes, Daddy, we will," Romaine said, beginning to cry.

"I'll be praying for you all." With that he turned and gave Mom one last hug and kiss as she wiped her eyes. There was always risk in these long treks.

We waved goodbye to Dad and Uncle Don from the porch as they and the ten carriers trudged down toward the lake. For the next few months our tie with him would be short-wave radio and infrequent letters. We didn't know when we'd see him again. It would depend on when he and Uncle Don could get an airstrip ready for us all to land on. I was the oldest, and expected to be helpful to Mom. I thought I could do that, but never imagined how hard it would be.

One day we had a visit from Ken Troutman, the mission leader. I came into the house after him, and everyone was somber, sitting in the tiny living room. He cleared his throat. "Peggy, we just received a telegram that your mother Sue Bowman died of a heart attack two days ago." I watched Mom's face fill with grief. She leaned forward and began sobbing uncontrollably, her shoulders shaking. Uncle Ken put his hand on her back.

"My mom's gone," she sobbed. "I won't get to be at her funeral, or see her on furlough! Never, never again on earth."

I began to tear up, and Romaine looked sad, sitting beside me. She hardly remembered Grandma, but I did. We had worn all the pretty dresses she had made. I so wished Dad could be here to comfort Mom. He was far away. If only we could make it to Grandma's funeral, to be with the other relatives and comfort one another.

Ken Troutman kept his hand on Mom's shoulder and prayed. "Oh Lord, please be very near to Peggy. You are the Comforter who helps us in each distress. Meet my sister in her deepest need."

After Uncle Ken left I hugged Mom, sitting on the couch. And I tried to be of help to her. Danny was starting to crawl, so I could watch him, dry dishes, make beds. But she wept often, and soon afterwards developed a bone infection in her thumb, and even with antibiotics it was very painful. She cried each time she lit and pumped the kerosene Tilly lamp at night. I prayed for Mom, prayed for us all, and especially that Dad would come home soon.

One Sunday we all crossed Lake Paniai on motorboats for a celebration in Obano where a brand new CMA airplane was to be dedicated. We enjoyed the dedication service and were going to have a picnic at a small beach on the way back. But rainy weather cancelled the picnic. I was so disappointed as we rode home in the motorboat, covered in a raincoat. "I'm sorry, Honey," Mom said. "We can't have a picnic in the middle of a downpour."

I knew she was right, but wondered why God had allowed rain when I had prayed for sunny weather.

The next day we awoke to see a large cloud of smoke rise from Obano.

"What's happening over there?" Ro asked.

"I don't know," Mom answered, "but I'll find out."

Other missionaries joined us on the hill, and when news came we were horrified. An Ekari rebel group had ambushed the plane and killed two local policemen and three Indonesian mission workers, including

Romaine's young playmate. The tribespeople had been planning to attack on Sunday, but decided to delay because of wet weather.

I was in awe. "Mom, all of us might have been killed yesterday, if the weather had been sunny. God protected us!"

"Yes, Marlene, that's true. He sent the rain. But I feel so bad for the families of those who were killed," Mom answered, wiping her eyes.

The uprising spread, and we were told to be on high alert. All the mission workers began sleeping in the big log house at night, with our bags packed. The Ekari were making war against all outsiders. Dutch soldiers were flown into the interior to protect their colony (Dutch New Guinea) and all foreigners.

I felt vulnerable even though we prayed as a family, and Mom talked to Dad on the radio often. I so wished Dad were here, but he and Uncle Don were days of jungle walking away, making contact with Danis.

There was comfort, however, in a black Scofield Bible Mom allowed me to read. It was one of Dad's Bibles and I was reading it for myself. Starting in Genesis I inched my way to Leviticus and bogged down. But I kept praying, "Lord, please keep Dad and Uncle Don. Please stop the rain in the Ilaga so the airstrip will dry up and a plane can land." We all prayed. Being nine and the oldest I continued to long for Dad to come home, especially for Christmas.

He didn't make it in time for Christmas, but God did answer my prayers. The uprising was quelled, we slept in our own log house again, and Mom's thumb healed. And soon the day arrived for us to actually fly to the Ilaga Valley to join Dad. What a miracle answer! It had been seven long months.

BARK HOUSE

That February morning of 1957 we rose in the early dawn, dressing quickly. Our possessions were all packed, carried down to the motorboats, and then we chugged across the blue lake in the misty morning. We were going to the Ilaga Valley, to our new home where Dad would be!

Two Missionary Aviation Fellowship planes sped down the grassy Obano airstrip, bearing our family and the Gibbonses aloft. Romaine and

I watched from the small plane's windows in wonder. We soared over ranges of jagged peaks, green valleys, puffy clouds. We finally descended into a broad but deep valley with a slanting airstrip on the edge of a forest, at elevation of 7,000 feet. We landed, bumping up the white sandy strip. Climbing out, shouting joyous Danis greeted us. I scanned the crowd, looking for Dad. He was there! But he had a beard now!

"Welcome to the Ilaga," he shouted over the crowd."

"Oh Dad, I've missed you so," I said.

He hugged and kissed us, tickling with his beard, then held Danny aloft for the Danis to see. Don Gibbons was laughing as well, as he greeted Aunt Alice and his girls Kathy and Joyce.

We all took pictures, waved the pilots goodbye, then trooped down the plateau into the valley toward the small bark-sided house Dad had built. We were happy and hungry in the thin air. Brown skinned Danis thronged us, singing their chanting songs. They were a warrior tribe with bows and arrows, and the men looked fierce. They wore head nets decorated with feathers and flowers, and pig tusks or bamboo pierced their noses. Many faces were painted black or red or striped. The women were mostly naked. Their bare tops were covered with colorful beads, and they wore short string or dried grass skirts. The children were naked, although girls sometimes wore a little grass skirt.

We trudged down a steep hill and through a village of round thatched roofs. Across more fields through which a tiny stream flowed. I saw the brown bark house in the distance-- tin-roofed and two storied, with glass paned windows winking at me, set back against a tall grassy hill. The outside was rough, the inside smooth, with pole framing. It was like a large rustic dollhouse….and it was our new home! We lunched on bread, peanut butter and cheese at the table Dad had built. But the table was so tall, we laughed. "Dad you'll have to cut the legs shorter!"

After lunch Romaine and I went upstairs to our bedroom to look out the open window at the thronging Danis. They were curious to see white children for the first time, and I made faces at them to make them laugh. Nine years old, outgoing, a new culture to make friends in…I was exhilarated.

That night we all prayed, thanking God together. He was faithful to our family—and to the Danis.

In the weeks following I acquainted myself with young native friends, especially Kurim, who was about my age. Romaine and I slowly picked up words, repeating them over and over, then put them into simple sentences. I pointed to some rattan jungle rope.

"Mun," Kurim told me.

"Mun," I repeated. "Ndi mun atet." (This is jungle rope.)

"Eo," she laughed. "Yes."

"Ti Lani Mende," I told her, pointing to my brother Danny. He had been given that name, meaning "of the Dani."

"Eo," Kurim answered. "Ti Lani Kwe (Dani Girl), she said, pointing to Romaine, nde kat Amengadu Mende Kwe (Girl from the Airstrip)" She pointed to me. Over the next months we picked up so many simple sentences that I could follow the jist of some conversations.

With Kurim and other young friends Romaine and I took afternoon walks west to a swift running stream, or climbed the tall hill behind us where there were glorious views of the valley.

Dad had begun construction on a larger frame house nearby that would be our permanent home. He drew me a small house plan of the layout of the rooms, which I saved. At dusk, as Danis built small fires in the yard, I gathered with them for warmth and closeness. They baked sweet potatoes and steamed bundles of spinach. Mom also boiled spinach for supper, and often we fried taro root—kom the natives called it. Delicious—as was the turtle meat flown in from the coast.

On Sundays large crowds gathered in the field in front of the bark house, and after tribal singing and dancing to repetitive worship refrains Dad would preach Bible stories in Moni, and a bilingual Dani would translate them. About the Great Spirit above all spirits, about creation, the fall of man, about a Savior who came to heal, redeem. The Danis were curious, and clan leaders held discussions afterwards.

Mom began homeschooling us again. I was behind in fourth grade, Romaine in second, so every weekday morning we worked on our lessons upstairs. I so wanted to be out playing with friends, exploring and learning more of the Dani language and ways. So we worked hard, and when lessons were done after lunch, we were free.

TRIBAL WARFARE

Dani war cries resounded from the hill beside our bark house one morning when Ro and I were doing our homework. Looking out the upstairs window I saw a band of men on the hill west of us shouting to villagers below, defying them. Our local Danis were responding with loud shouts. Their cries rang out to villages up and down the valley, warning them of danger, calling them to war. Each message ended with whoops that sounded like big exclamation points.

Men were running together forming small bands, armed with bows and arrows, long spears, war jackets. Many of the warriors had their head nets decorated with feathers or small flowers, with their faces painted red or black. The air was electric with tribal fervor.

Dad went outside to investigate and came back in with Jimbitu, a friendly Dani leader who was bilingual. Jimbitu wore a woven string head net with a pig tusk and bird feathers adorning it. Though his face was painted black, with a pig tusk through his nose, his expression was benevolent. He had flowers stuck into his rattan upper armbands, a shell necklace and small chest net. And of course he had the gourd that all men wore for modesty. It was interesting to me that Dani men adorned themselves so much more than the women.

"Jimbitu says the Danis who were pushed out of the valley in Taganit's War have come to fight and get their land back, with reinforcements of Damal and Dugwa tribes. There have been three other skirmishes in the past two years with over 100 killed," Dad informed us.

I didn't know anything about Taganit's War, but I knew war was terrible.

"There are now about 120 up toward the airstrip. The people here are uniting to fight against them." Dad declared.

"Will we be safe?" Mom questioned.

Jimbitu assured us in Moni, "These enemy are not against you. They are fighting against the ones who took their land."

I watched as Dad loaded the shotgun he kept on hand. "Just in case we need it," he explained. "But we should pray."

As Jimbitu left, a few of our Moni and Ekari helpers from other valleys gathered in our little house. One of them began to intercede fervently—we all bowed our heads. "Oh God, protect us. Help the warriors to go home, and the fighting to stop. We are your children."

"Yes, Lord," I agreed with him. It was dangerous...but I loved excitement.

We went outside, watching the warriors from our tribe shout and race northwest toward the fight. The enemy band by then had fled backwards toward the airstrip, and into the forest.

A couple of hours later a young Dani warrior came into our yard, clearly in distress. His shoulder muscle was pierced with a barbed arrow. You could see both ends. "They are continuing to fight in the forest," he panted. "Can you help me?"

Dad found pliers and carefully pulled the jagged piece of wood out, while the young man clenched his teeth, but made no sound. The Danis were terribly brave, I decided. Mom applied antiseptic and bandage carefully. "Kayonak, kayonak," the warrior kept repeating. "Thank you, thank you." And he headed back to the fight.

Later in the day after rain Dad decided to head up the hill and see if he could help any other wounded men. All the enemy had been pushed back, we heard, so there was no danger.

"Can I go too, Dad?"

Dad hesitated a moment, then said, "Sure!"

My tennis shoes squished on the muddy uphill trail as I scampered after Dad and another Dani. Scattered trees gave way to low bushes of the higher plateau, all wet from the recent shower. White rhododendrons bobbed in the damp breeze. The sky was washed clean, the sun trying to break through low clouds. I turned around. The broad valley below looked peaceful, villages scattered across it with smoky mist rising from dark thatched roofs. What would we find ahead?

We heard Dani voices calling us to come over to a nearby village. "An enemy is lying here. Come and see," one shouted. Trudging over we found a man lying face down outside the fence. Villagers were watching, some leaning over the rough fence to watch his shallow breaths. I saw that a spear had pierced his back, and there were many arrow wounds on his body. He seemed unconscious.

Dad leaned over him and spoke comforting words. "Nore," he called him. "Friend." The Danis snickered. This man was not their friend. Dad put his hand on his shoulder, and prayed sincerely for him in Dani. The man didn't respond. I felt so bad for him.

We finally left the dying man and trekked north toward the airstrip where we met a few warriors heading home—others were still fighting the scattered enemy in the high forest. These men were naked, Dad later told me, because Danis take off their gourds when they go to war. I hadn't noticed. But there were four bodies lying by the edge of the airstrip. Dad told me to wait while he went to check on them.

"Yes, they're dead," he affirmed when he returned. "No way to help them."

"It's so sad, Dad."

"Yes, it really is, Marlene. We need to pray for their families, and for peace."

None of them knew the Lord, I thought. So many tribal peoples live their lives sacrificing pigs to evil spirits for protection. And these four men died that way. Without knowing Jesus.

We found out later that 33 of the enemy died in that skirmish and two of our Ilaga Danis. The land they lived in was defended. But 35 families suffered anguish because their loved one passed away, and they had no hope of ever seeing him again.

This is why we are here in the Ilaga Valley, I knew. My parents were living among this tribe so they could hear of Jesus and eternal life. I was proud of the Dani. Someday I would grow up to be a missionary also. God would send me to another tribe like them.

CULTURE SHOCK

We had only been four months among the Dani as a family, and then it was time to return to the States—our four year term was ended.

"Dad, why can't we stay longer in the Ilaga? We're just settling in, and you're building our new house. And the Danis are just beginning to hear about Jesus."

"Well, Marlene, first term missionaries only stay four years, then five each following term. The mission wants each family to go home for a year to rest, tell churches about our work, and sometimes to get more training. We get to be with all our relatives, too.

"That will be special," I agreed.

Mom hurried us through our Calvert Course lessons so Romaine and I would complete second and fourth grades. One of my assignments was to write a long essay.

What should I write about, I wondered? The war on the airstrip? That would be interesting —no one else would be writing about something like that. And if I wrote it well the teacher might give me an A!

I worked hard on the paper, hopeful that the teacher grading me in the States would enjoy the unusual story. "You did a good job, Marlene," Mom said, smiling.

Dad continued to build a larger tin-roofed frame house across the field, finishing one room upstairs so we could store our belongings in it. Mom packed, mailed off our homework assignments, and we said goodbye to our Dani friends.

My first impression of America was how clean and well ordered it looked--with wide roads, big stores, big houses. So strange, so different from the Ilaga Valley.

We unpacked in a three bedroom duplex across from Aunt Christine and Uncle Maxey in Livonia, Michigan. Dad was going to attend the University of Michigan at Ann Arbor, and Romaine and I would walk six blocks to Rosedale School.

Mom and Dad bought us bicycles, and we practiced riding up and down the street. We watched black and white TV for the very first time at our cousin Ken's house, enjoying the Mickey Mouse Club. We often visited the library where I could check out all sorts of books—but I was told my limit was ten. Over the months I read books by the dozens, absorbing pioneer stories, adventures, biographies.

When school started I tried to fit in, to be a normal fifth grader. But this was my first time in a regular classroom. In the beginning I was quiet and observant. My teacher Mr. Wright, a slight thin man, sensed my struggle and was kind and helpful. I began to love school and want to excel.

On Sundays we drove an hour to the CMA Central Church in downtown Detroit, then in the evenings often attended a Baptist church nearer us. I listened attentively to sermons, taking church seriously. Some sermons were interesting, some boring.

Once I asked Dad, "Why does the pastor at the Baptist church give altar calls for salvation after all his sermons? The people who attend on Sunday night are Christians, people that he knows."

"That's a good question," Dad answered. "Maybe you should ask him."

I never followed through with asking the pastor, but I was hungry to learn more of God.

On May 1, 1958 our family celebrated a brand new baby into the family. David was born in Ann Arbor, and when he came home we all wanted to hold him. Tiny, with pinpricks of blond hair, he was adorable. Danny was two, so now Romaine and I could help Mom by each caring for one brother.

One day Mom and Dad received a telegram from Ken Troutman the field chairman in New Guinea. They had already read it when we arrived home from school, and were sober.

"Our new framed house in the Ilaga is all burned down. So our outfit is mostly gone. Just what's packed in drums might be usable," Mom told us brokenly.

"How did that happen?" I asked amazed "Did someone start the fire?"

"It might be spontaneous combustion," Dad answered. "If it got real hot in that finished room, and there were any rags with kerosene on them, maybe fumes would ignite sawdust, or cardboard. But perhaps an angry Dani lit fire. I can't think of any native being that angry against us."

"Dad, the chime clock might be burned up, and our books and toys," Romaine burst out.

"Yes, that's true. We don't know if anything's saved. We'll have to reorder another outfit, and raise money for it. I pray my field notes and the beginning Dani dictionary are saved." Dad leaned on his knees and put his face in his hands. "So much work is lost, if they're burned."

In evening devotions we all prayed for the Danis and for any of our outfit that could be salvaged back in the Ilaga. And for God to provide what we needed to go back to live in New Guinea the next five years.

As summer arrived Mom and Dad packed and shipped drums of clothes, bedding, books, and kitchen supplies. And they prepared Romaine and I for change.

"There's a new grade school being started in Sentani for all of the missionary kids," Mom told us. "You girls will join others to be in the very first class, and you'll get to stay in a dorm house with other kids. They'll have fun activities, and you'll get to go to the beach sometimes."

"How often will we come home?" I asked.

"Every summer for three months, and a month at Christmas. And we'll fly out to see you in the middle of the school term, also."

"That sounds like fun, being with other kids in a dorm," I said thoughtfully. "And we'll be together, Ro."

"Yeah, we would still be roommates, only with others."

"Sentani is where it's so tropical, like Biak. There'll be palm trees and cicadas singing loud on hot afternoons."

Romaine nodded. She remembered.

BOARDING SCHOOL

Romaine and I were excited to be joining a new school where Aunt Betty was our young but capable housemother. She was 26 and attractive, with a sturdy figure and a good sense of humor. There were only five students in the beginning: Beverly Boggs and her brother Barton, Romaine and me, and Larry Lake. Beverly and I were the oldest, in sixth grade. In months to come others joined us, and after three years when I graduated from eighth grade there were eighteen.

I imagine Mom and Dad had mixed feelings when they left their two oldest on the coast. Mom was close to tears. Though they still had Danny and David with them, which blunted the loss, we never after that all lived long in one place together, except for our next furlough.

"Goodbye, Marlene," Mom said, hugging me close, then moved to Romaine. "We'll be praying for you every day, and writing often."

"Keep up the good schoolwork," Dad encouraged, his arm around my shoulders. "We're so proud of you girls. We'll come out soon to visit."

Ro and I waved them goodbye as they were driven down the hill, then turned and ran across the ravine to class. This is what missionary kids do, I thought. I would adjust to life in two places.

I had a sense of expectation and eagerness to grow in my new tropical landscape. There was also a sense of loss in not being able to plunge into life with the Danis again and pick up the language. But I consoled myself I would make the best of our vacation times at home. We did miss much of Dan and David's preschool years, however. They were brothers from a distance… and we had to work at growing closer in the few months we were with them each year.

In fact, our brothers had opportunity to be immersed in Dani life in a way Romaine and I never were. When they finally left for boarding school Dan and Dave knew Dani fluently—and David even spoke English with an accent!

I grew to love Sentani, living there eight months of the year, but home was really among the Danis where Mom and Dad were. We would each brag about our parents or tribe and valley, knowing our home was the best, and Aunt Betty would quietly smile.

Living on Sentani hill, tin roofed houses baked under the hot sun, and grasses waved as wind blew over the rocky hillside and the cement slabs Allied troops had left after serving under General MacArthur during World War II. On the slab above our residence we played ball, hopscotch, and roller skated. Across a small ravine was our schoolhouse where Miss Heikkenen read us stories of Hiawatha and Minnehaha after our lessons were done.

Having pioneered Dalat School for missionary kids in Viet Nam years ago, Miss Heikkenen had a wealth of teaching experience. She was in her 50's, dark haired with glasses, stood very erect, and taught with good discipline. She knew how to teach several grades at once with order and good humor. We loved her with enough awe to work hard at our lessons.

Every evening after supper and showers we gathered around Aunt Betty for devotions. First she read a fun story out of Star of Light or Treasures of the Snow, or The Tanglewoods Secret (by Patricia St. John). When she read Little Pilgrim's Progress, we were glad when Christian lost his burden at the cross, concerned as he made his way across the Slough of Despond, and horrified as he descended into the Valley of Humiliation. "Will Self kill Christian?" Larry asked.

"No," I answered "He has to live to make it to the Celestial City!"

After a vivid Bible story with pertinent questions at the end we all prayed. There was security and routine. Each Sunday we wrote a letter to our parents, and in turn received letters back. Usually once every term our parents would fly out to visit. And we would stay with them in a vacation house, exulting in holiday freedom.

Often on Saturdays we piled into the red jeep and Aunt Betty drove us the 30 or so miles to Hollandia (now Jayapura) for an outing. As the paved road wound through the jungle we watched for the red streaks of flame of the forest foliage, loved the shrieks of tropical birds. We could spend our allowance at a toko run by a Chinese man, then usually went swimming at Base G, where Allied tankers were lined up, rusting since the war. Sticky and sandy we drove to a primitive restaurant and munched on lumpias, delicious greasy eggrolls filled with meat and vegetables. Home at last after driving through the starlight we showered, had devotions, and fell into our bunks.

On Sundays all of the mission workers gathered at the large home down the hill where various missionaries would preach. Some were interesting, some longwinded and boring. I liked Uncle Harold Catto the best—he was lively, funny, and applied the Bible teaching clearly.

These grades school years Romaine and I had on the coast rounded our cultural experience in American life. The classroom teaching was excellent, and there was a godly environment at the dorm with Aunt

Betty. There was even a sense of comraderie with the other MK's. We were all in this unusual extended family life together, with our parents on the frontier preaching the Gospel. And if Mom had continued homeschooling us, we would have had a much harder time adapting to the States next furlough....I would have been a Dani with an American education.

However, the downside was that—really, no one understood like Mom or Dad. There were corners of my heart that didn't get met and couldn't fully be expressed in a letter. Deep expression of family life waited until I went home on school break.

CHRISTMAS TREE

The high point of every year at Sentani School was flying home for Christmas. This December morning of 1958 we woke before dawn, because Aunt Betty had gifts for us to unwrap before leaving.

I unwrapped my gifts and squealed with joy. "Aunt Betty, I love it! Such a tiny red tomato pincushion--I can use it as I sew! Thanks so much." I hugged her neck, and Beverly did too. She had gotten one just like mine.

"And we love the scarf and necklace," Beverly added.

Aunt Betty smiled. "I picked them out just for you."

Romaine and I carried our suitcases and gifts to the jeep and all of us jounced down to the airstrip where MAF planes awaited to fly each set of siblings to their destination. Waving good bye, we roared down the runway and took off into clear blue sky. Sentani became a miniature town with scattered houses, and climbing higher we crossed range after range of steep mountains. It was cold in the plane, the air was thinner...we huddled in our jackets....and then after an hour or more we circled and landed down into our own Ilaga Valley.

Home! The sweetest place on earth, with Mom and Dad, Danny and David waving, then hugging us, and Danis whooping as we trekked down to the newly built house. On the way we detoured into the forest. "Where are we going, Dad?" I asked. "This is not the trail to our house."

"I thought we'd cut our Christmas tree on the way home," Dad answered. "You girls are here now, so we should pick it out together."

"Great," I exclaimed. "I love the walking in the forest."

We found one that Romaine claimed was just right, and Dan helped Dad carry it after he sawed it down. David was on the back of a native, being carried.

Our new home was larger, across the field from the bark house, with three rooms downstairs, a bath-shower alcove, and four bedrooms up. We still had the outhouse, but now it was in our enclosed backyard, so we didn't have to pass clusters of natives during the day. Romaine and my bedroom faced east, down valley, where we could watch the rain coming in the afternoons. The house was painted light green with dark green boards to accent, and a lattice fence bordering the flower beds. Rain on the metal roof could lull us to sleep at night, and become our drinking water as it ran into long gutters that flowed into a holding tank. So now we even had running water!

Mom had a dinner for us, cooked on the black woodstove—sliced, fried beef with Dani greens, baked sweet potatoes to add butter and salt to. Crisp carrots to crunch on. Why did food taste better at home?

We showered at night, filling a large bucket with woodstove heated water, pulling the bucket high on a pulley, and fastening the rope tightly. With a quick turn of the sprinkler at its base, the shower started. Rinsing at the end was luxurious—but you had to have saved enough water.

Setting up the tree in the living room, we decorated it with balls, homemade ornaments, and silvery icicles. As there was no electricity, there were no Christmas lights. After the Bible story and prayer I climbed the stairs with a kerosene lantern to our bedroom. "Goodnight Mom, Goodnight, Dad." I loved reading at night by lamplight. A "Dani" girl at home, with the Ilaga River a distant roar deep in the valley. I snuggled under thick covers--it was cold in the high altitude. All over the valley Danis carried coals from their fires upstairs to their small attic bedroom. Coals warmed them, covers warmed me. All of us were sleeping warm.

This was our first Christmas in the Ilaga as a family, and each year it was celebrated over several days. We would gather with the Gibbons family (or the Ellenburgers, in later years) to sing carols, open gifts, and banquet. Another day would be the big pig feast the Danis held, with the exchange of gifts of pork, dance to worship songs, and the nativity story preached--and even enacted--in years to come.

Our family Christmas began in the early morning, as in the States, with all four of us kids opening the pile of gifts under the tree. Boxes of presents had been shipped months before by all of the relatives, and Mom and Dad had added to them. "Just what I wanted," I exclaimed, as I lifted out a pretty blouse," or "Oh, no....Aunt Imogene sent Romaine and me flannel pajamas again!"

"But they're a larger size, and warm for the weather here, Honey."

"I know, Mom, but they're so plain."

"But Aunt Imogene means well," Ro piped in. "She probably just doesn't know what else to send." Ro was often more grateful and content than me. Dan and David were occupied playing with new Tonka Toy cars, rolling them back and forth on the wooden floor.

We had a real turkey for dinner, roasted a golden brown—flown in frozen from Australia. And oranges, and apples, a crate of each, that would be savored for weeks. We were allowed one a day, an enormous treat.

How rich we were! I felt especially blessed at Christmas. Compared to the Dani people we lived like kings. We had meat every day, medicine when we needed it, even Tilly pump lights at night. A kerosene refrigerator. Clothes to keep us warm. And most of all, we had the Bible...we knew God. Jesus lived in our hearts by His Spirit.

TWO LIVES

For the next three years Romaine and I travelled back and forth between the Ilaga Valley and Sentani School. It was like living on two different continents, but we began to think it was normal.

The first few nights in Sentani, kids would sob quietly in their bunk beds for parents back home. But as the days passed, the school routine and renewed friendships lulled our loneliness. We adjusted. Aunt Betty Johnson, Miss Heikkenen, and later Miss Randall always tried to make us feel welcome and valued.

As the school grew in numbers Beverly and I were moved to a small extra bedroom built onto the main house. Palm branches waved over our tin roof at night, making a swishing sound. "Do you hear that sound, Bev? It almost sounds like waves on the ocean."

"I know, I love it," Bev answered sleepily.

"I wish we could read in bed here. At home I always read by kerosene light late at night."

"Uh-huh. That would be nice. But they want us to wake up early." Bev rolled over on the bunk above me, drifting off to sleep.

Moonlight slid across our cement floor…tropical nights were glorious. I decided that when I grew older I would be sure to sleep outside in the moonlight.

Loving to read, I slowly checked out all the interesting books our school library possessed, and when I came across a children's edition of Lorna Doone, I caught my breath. "This is the same book that the Troutmans had loaned me in Enarotali," I thought. "They must have donated it." It was a blue, hardback, illustrated with vivid drawings.

"Miss Heikkenen, would you let me trade Lorna Doone for this other book I have? I read this copy years ago."

"Certainly, Marlene." She smiled.

I reread the romance and any others I could get hold of, and began making up stories at night in bed. Stories I would write someday, if I remembered them.

History was fascinating, especially tales of the Middle Ages. I wrote a story of Lady Rose and her Page Oakley for Mom and Dad, for a future Christmas gift.

As an scholastic incentive, Miss Heikkenen developed a race around the schoolroom, tacking up outpost station names on the four walls. Whoever got a 100% on any math lesson would move their airplane from one station to the next. Choosing to win the race, I made sure my math work was perfect—and I won!

I tried hard to be perfect, began to be obsessive about certain routines…washing, cleaning my desk. I was lonely, yet working hard to please. Aunt Betty was special, but not my mother. And I missed my dad, his understanding and wisdom.

Every holiday at home cured this, for a time. We would have happy, laughing meals around the table at night. Lively discussions on many topics--and controversy was allowed. I noticed that my dad did not mind being contradicted, if I could prove my point logically. He liked his children to think clearly. He was a linguist, anthropologist, a researcher. And during these years he was gathering data on cycles of warfare among the Danis in the valley, working toward his PhD.

GOSPEL BREAKTHROUGH

Every three month summer break and four week Christmas break when we were home, I saw how busy Mom and Dad were. The emphasis on evangelism eventually turned into concentration on discipleship and beginning a basic Bible school for new pastors. And there was the ongoing work of Bible translation ever before Dad. Mom developed primers to teach the Danis how to read, and raised up new leader/readers to teach reading and writing in their communities.

The gospel breakthrough with the Dani tribe began soon after furlough. Obalalok and his clan decided to burn their fetishes and turn to follow the Great Creator like the Damal tribe near them. They lived in two villages totaling about 200 people.

A Sunday was set, and upon a long wooden pyre men, women, and children placed sacred objects that symbolized the appeasement they had made to evil spirits by killing pigs. There were tails of pigs sewn onto string carrying bags, strings of cowrie shells, sacred arrows, and stones that were rubbed onto young boys during initiation ceremonies. Individuals took off charms from their neck or arms that were to protect them from evil spirits, laying them also on the pyre. As the wood was lit the Danis watched, then began dancing in a big circle, singing their chants of worship to God.

This symbolic—yet concrete---break with their animistic past was a huge step of faith. The Damal across the valley had burned their fetishes—now Obalalok and his clan were following. Would they be safe? Other Dani clans watched, considered, and there were long discussions in the field below our house after Sunday services.

The services themselves were amazing. When I was home, Sunday was my favorite day of the week. Across the valley you could hear clans approaching as they sang their way along, running and dancing down the paths. Each clan would announce their arrival with a long string of warriors spiraling onto the hard-baked field below our house, singing and dancing until the circle was huge. The worship refrains were repeated over and over. As more arrived the melded group might change the pattern and run east and west, singing. And sometimes they did a two-step that had a stronger beat to it. The men would hit their bows and arrows on their legs, for emphasis.

I loved the action, the singing, and joined them. Romaine and I would dance, and Danny would run...David join in on the shoulders of a native. After a length of gathering, the masses of people would sit on the hard ground, men and women separately.

In the beginning when the Danis all gathered in one place, the basic truths of the gospel were taught in story form. Until my father had learned enough Dani, he used a Moni interpreter. But with the large crowd of a thousand or more, their voices were not loud enough. So sometimes men were set in a larger perimeter around the central preachers, and they would relay the interpretation. All this took time, but the people were patient. Crying children were shushed or carried further out of the crowds. If rain came the people scattered, but other times the men stayed after the service and clan leaders discussed whether they might turn to the Jesus way...or bring up an issue of who stole some pigs, who had rights to a certain garden plot, etc. As more clans burned fetishes to follow the gospel, the discussions turned to practical theology and how these truths might best be applied to their lives.

I was fascinated with how the chiefs, the clan leaders would orate and make their point. Most of the men were decorated with the ususal bird feathers and flowers on their head nets, had pig tusks through their noses. Their faces were painted black, red, or striped. Their armbands often had bamboo or flowers stuck in them, and their gourd (penis sheath) might be long or short. A chief usually was brightly decorated-- but not always. His strong demeanor gave him away. With a voice resonant and eloquent, his forceful reasoning was amplified with expressive arm flourishes. Strong point made, he would sit down, and another leader would stand to agree or refute him.

These large gatherings were unwieldy, so in time as more and more clans followed Jesus, my parents formed a Bible school where each area could send a couple to be their pastor. These couples would learn the gospel principles and stories and teach them each Sunday to their villages. In this way new churches were started across the valley, and each clan received personal attention.

Since the New Testament pattern was for a pastor to have only one wife, sadly no chief could be a pastor. Chiefs, tribal leaders, typically had two to four wives. They had amassed enough riches to buy more than one, and each wife working hard produced more food, children, and pigs to grow more wealth. Chiefs thus gave the feasts out of their wealth…but they could not pastor. The leaders understood this, and sent their brightest young couples—often a chief's son, who could be trained as the community pastor.

In time there were about 20 young Dani couples in the Bible Witness School who attended classes Mom and Dad taught weekday mornings. The men then taught the Bible stories and lessons to their scattered churches throughout the valley…and our family would take turns visiting each one. I loved the trekking, the picnicking, sitting in the hot sun among crowds of Danis worshipping, listening to the Bible stories made relevant to the tribe. I often wore a head net slung down my back, sometimes painted my forehead with a stripe of black. I even developed a crush on Wejak our house helper!

Romaine and I helped Mom and Dad during these vacations. We hung wet clothes on clotheslines on wash day, then snatched them off quickly as afternoon rain arrived. I helped press clothes with the heavy kerosene powered iron, and learned to make bread, cinnamon rolls, even pies. And in the early years before a nurse arrived in the valley I took bandages, sulfa salve and iodine to the back porch, to clean and wrap wounds, and applied eye ointment. This was my job…I was going to be a nurse someday! "Labogo, labogo," the Danis thanked me, clasping my hand.

As more of the population learned to read, one summer Mom needed help. "Could you check the readers as they come, Marlene? If they pass one primer, I give them the next one. But I have to be sure they can truly read the one they have."

"Sure, Mom." Some read quickly and clearly...others were slower, stumbling over syllables and words. One lady who failed the test wept, and I felt so sorry for her. In her culture she felt humiliated. Older adults sometimes were slower in learning than the young people.

During afternoon naptime I would scour our bookshelves for interesting books. There were a few classics like David Copperfield, and The House of Seven Gables, some interesting missionary biographies, and a number of anthropology resources, especially ones by Margaret Meade. So I could compare the Danis to her descriptions of tribal life in other places.

I saw that cultures were amazingly diverse. And I was immersed in two of them. The exotic warlike Dani culture colored my life vividly four months out of the year. And the Larson home and boarding school life trained me in patterns of living. Through it all was God's Word, the life of the Holy Spirit teaching me, above culture and geography.

DANI HEARTH FIRE

A peaceful expectancy infuses the Dani men's house where I sit cross-legged, watching the fire. The round thatched men's house in the Ilaga Valley in Irian Jaya feels warm and smoke scented. As the embers twinkle red and gold Tabeme the chief of this community sitting across from me stirs the coals and adds chunks of wood.

I breathe deeply with contentment. My father is sitting along the wall behind Tabeme, a Dani preacher near him. Dad's tanned frame does not blend into the shadows like the preacher's dark one. They are interviewing candidates for next week's large baptism. As one man exits the small door near Dad, another steps in and sits on the soft hay.

The preacher makes note of the man's name and questions him. "Who is God, and why did he send his Son to earth?"

He is the Great Creator, and he sent Jesus to be the sacrifice for our wrong doings," he answers. "So now we don't have to sacrifice our pigs to appease the evil spirits."

"Are you trusting in God's Son to save you? Are you going to forsake the old ways and not wear the sacred charms to ward off bad spirits?

"Eo," the man nods his assent.

After a few more questions he leaves, and I watch Tabeme the chief. It was at his insistence that my father agreed to bring our family this weekend to camp in the village of Erongobak.

A few days earlier Tabeme had become exasperated with my father. "I have asked you many times to come to our village and check our people so we can be baptized with the Eromaga clan next week." He was standing in our kitchen by the woodstove. "You have said, 'We will come.' But now the Eromaga clans will be baptized without us—and we want to be included. Remember—when you first came to the Ilaga Valley it was my clan who you camped among, and we made sure you and your carriers had enough sweet potatoes and greens. I took care of you like a father. And now you have not included us in this large baptism."

My father apologized to this small, forceful man. Tabeme was not adorned as many chiefs were with bird feathers on his head net, a pig tusk through his nose, or flowers in his armbands. A simple head net framed his mahogany face, but his intelligent eyes and direct speech portrayed authority.

"You indeed did feed us, Tabeme," my dad had answered. "Your strong care made a way for us to be welcomed in the rest of the Ilaga. I have just been busy. So many people come with requests, and there are planes to meet, and I have been putting Scriptures into the Dani language. It takes much time."

"Yes, but we are among your first people, your near clansmen. We must also be gathered into this baptism. We also are on the forefront."

"Again, I confess my overlooking you," Dad answered humbly. "You are like my father, and I honor you. My whole family will come and camp in your main village. Have your people ready, each to be questioned with your clan preacher."

Now in the men's house I watch Tabeme sitting with his arms crossed over his knees, relaxed and benevolent. His insistence on pressing forward in the Kingdom with his whole clan into baptism makes me admire him. His three wives have already been interviewed, accepted for baptism.

Now another man and his two wives enter to be questioned. They all want to follow the Jesus way and have burned their sacred charms. They all took the risk that their children will not die, their pigs and gardens will keep producing, and no harm will come to them. And as they stopped sacrificing to evil spirits, they are trusting the Great Creator for protection. Other clans in the valley will be watching.

Occasionally the fire crackles. The embers glow deep red. I take a deep breath and realize how rich I am. Almost 13, home from boarding school, in the midst of my Dani tribe. Though blond-haired, I am a part of them--one with them. Inside I am Dani.

My family is here, and we are following Christ. My American family and Dani family are gathering into God's family. I myself will be baptized with them this weekend. This outward symbol of passing from death into life I am taking alone and we are taking together.

"Someday," I think to myself, "I will reach another tribe with the Gospel. My life will be immersed in bringing people to Jesus like Mom and Dad are." I sigh with satisfaction.

Over a two-year span there were 25 fetish burnings, and by the third year around that many churches established across the broad valley. Early on a band of Danis trekked down river to their relatives in the Grand Baliem, carrying the gospel, my Dad among them. Mom and Danny and David flew to join them—and Romaine and I heard from Sentani how many Danis in the Baliem were burning their charms and turning to the Lord. We were so happy...the revival was spreading.

THE PLANE RIDES

There was a special graduation ceremony for Beverly Boggs and me at the end of 8th grade, with Harold Catto the field chairman giving the exhortation. We were the first graduates of Sentani School! Mom and Dad beamed at the reception.

"We're so proud of you, Marlene. You're so grown up now! And almost as tall as me," Mom said, smiling. "Tomorrow we want to borrow the van and drive to Hollandia to shop for clothes for you for high school."

After a special holiday, I hugged the family close before boarding the two-engine plane, to fly to Dalat School in Viet-Nam. It was the only 1st through 12th grade school the CMA had in the Orient—and the mission was willing to pay for those long flights. I was both excited and a little scared.

Dad handed me my tickets and passport as we sat in the small airport lounge. "Here are a list of names, addresses and telephone numbers of all the destinations, and there will be someone to meet you at each airport. We'll be praying for you every day…remember, the Lord is with you."

"Thanks, Dad. I love you all!" I hugged him, Mom, Dad, and Ro and we cried some. I tickled Danny and David. At five and three they would be more grown up when I came home. "I'll bring you souvenirs," I told them.

Viet Nam was far away. But it was better to go there to high school than back to the States for three years. Since the three month vacation for Dalat School was over Christmastime, I would be gone for four months, then come home for three months.

That day the plane to Biak was full of Dutch soldiers, and when I seated myself next to one blond uniformed man the others cheered and joked with him in Dutch. I smiled timidly. I changed planes at the familiar Biak airport, and we droned on across the ocean.

Almost fourteen, I felt both mature and unsure of myself. Thankfully, Mrs. Coles met me at the Manila Airport, and even took me shopping during my five-day stay at the CMA guest home. I found Philippine souvenirs for the family and mailed them back as a surprise…then boarded the plane for Bangkok.

The guest home in Bangkok looked familiar. It was the same white pillared mansion I had stayed at when five years old! And there I met about thirty other MKs whose parents had dropped them off for their journey to Dalat School.

What a joy. I began to make friends, and we trooped onto the plane headed for Saigon with noisy confidence. One night at the Alliance Saigon guest home, then our band made the last flight to Dalat in a smaller airplane attended by delicate Vietnamese stewardesses in native dress. We were met by house parents in big vans who drove us through the provincial town and up a low hill to white buildings framed in pines—Dalat School.

The two-storied boys and girls dorms were connected by a large dining hall. Above that dining room some of the lady teachers and a nurse lived. Sports fields and teacher homes were scattered on the hills, with pine trees and flowers scenting the cool air.

I settled into a dorm room graced with four iron beds and two wooden dressers. My new roommates were in the 9th and 10th grades—all three friendly and cheerful. I was off to a good start.

But my strong confidence was short-lived. I had underestimated social differences. It had taken time to learn the culture and language of the Monis, the Danis, and Dalat School was no different. The school had about 120 kids, 1st grade through 12th, with about thirty of these in high school. A rather small school by American standards, it was large to me.

The teachers were of the same caliber as Sentani, dedicated professionals investing their lives to train missionary kids for God. And our house parents, Uncle Gene and Aunt Cleo Evans were caring mission workers who had left their fieldwork to oversee us teenaged girls. (Their daughter Joanne was also a 9th grader, assigned to a different dorm room.) But most of the students had been coming to Dalat since grade school from outposts in southeast Asia, and were already good friends. I was an outsider, and they were getting to know me.

I was not intimidated, however. Being a cheerful extrovert I participated in group activities and thought I was fitting in, until one small incident collapsed my confidence.

We had been relaxing in our dorm room, and out of boredom I began jouncing on my iron bed. It was springy...I kept bouncing up and down, up and down. It was childish but fun until one roommate began to deride me.

"Come on, Marlene—keep jumping! Keep bouncing!" It was a mocking tone...and others joined in, on and on.

I didn't know what to do. Embarrassed, I kept springing on the bed. The others finally quit the spiteful teasing and I stopped, and we left for supper when the bell rang. But the hurt remained...and there was no one to share my heart with. There was a subculture to this high school, that I hadn't caught on to yet. I was also learning how to dress, how to fix my hair, how to be cool.

I became quieter, observant, introspective. Aunt Cleo took notice of me, sometimes even offered to style my hair at night in rollers—and the next day my blond curls looked better! But the spurts of confidence were short lived.

There were no group devotions here at Dalat, but we did have Sunday church and in the evening, youth group. We were to have our own quiet times with the Lord. And I did. Sitting on my bed, leaning against the wall I would read the New Testament, searching for strength, comfort.

"I'm so lonely, Lord. Please help me." I sensed His presence. He was there. But somehow I didn't break through to fullness, completeness. My hurt was not healed.

Even in my schoolwork I didn't excel like I used to. Many in senior high were achievers who mostly made A's. I made B's...I was average, felt average.

Even below average.

The house parents were creative in sponsoring fun weekend activities. We had hikes and picnics, bonfires in the forest, outings to Dalat town, and many Friday night basketball games. Occasionally I had a date, but being self-conscious I hardly knew how to act.

Each semester break when I went home my emotional life swung upward. I was cherished, important to my parents, important among the Danis. I could be myself again.

One of the vacations though was so short—four weeks-- that all of the MK's from Indonesia and Irian Jaya stayed with the house parents and had a short holiday in Saigon. It was special, but that year I didn't see my family for nine months. Dad later commented on my emotional outlook after I finally arrived home. "We felt bad that you looked down a lot, Marlene...you didn't look up and face people. You were withdrawn."

"That's true, Dad. I've felt put down at Dalat. But when I come home I become happier and secure, among family and the Danis. I wish it could be different for me at high school."

"I do too. Maybe when Romaine comes with you, you can help each other."

My last year at Dalat was definitely better. Romaine was in ninth grade, I in eleventh, and though we lived in different parts of the dorm, we were family together.

I had been practicing clarinet—Dad had given me lessons over the summer. I continued music lessons at Dalat, and played at the annual recital in a new white dress. It was Mozart's concerto for clarinet in B flat, a lilting, haunting melody that he wrote soon before his death. The audience clapped loudly, and I smiled. Romaine was there beaming, but Mom and Dad weren't. As musicians themselves they would have been so proud.

During my last semester (the last half of 11th grade), I experienced serendipity. Or it could be called a unique answer to prayer. Dalat offered housing and the chapel to American officers and servicemen who wanted a spiritual retreat. These soldiers were stationed at different outposts in southern Viet Nam, so the cool highlands of Dalat were welcome to them. During one of the retreats Jack, a 19-year-old chaplain's assistant, took special interest in me. He was dark haired, good looking. We dated a little, then from Saigon he sent letters and candy.

My life brightened because of this love and attention. I was special to one young man! Also, Judy Whetzel and Judy Thompson and I began to hang out as good friends…the puzzle pieces of high school life began fitting into a cheerful picture, just as I was about to leave. Even so I was still glad that furlough was coming. In June Mom and Dad, Danny and David would visit Dalat and then we would all fly to the States for my senior year.

When Jack's deployment was over I said goodbye to him for the last time sadly. He was from California…I would be living in Livonia, Michigan.

ISRAEL, ROME, PARIS...

On our journey to the States I was filled with delight. I had loved European history—now we were going to actually visit places I had read about in books. Mom and Dad had decided we would reach America by travelling west instead of east. One of our first stops was Israel. We landed in Tel Aviv a few hours after the Beatles had left the airport, continuing on a world tour.

"How amazing," I said to Ro. "I wish we could have landed sooner and seen them!"

"Yeah," Ro answered. That would have been so cool."

We stayed at the YMCA Hotel in Jerusalem whose tall tower was a landmark, the massive stone building elegant, with stretching lawns. The spacious mosaic tiled lobby was staffed by Jordanians at that time. And there were the scriptural sites! The massive wall of the city, the Garden Tomb close to Golgotha hill with the face of the skull in it, the winding ancient bazaar streets. How amazing to walk where Jesus had once trudged! We meandered through the Garden of Gethsemane reflecting, drove up to the Mount of Olives, later bought souvenirs in Bethlehem, and small black urns in Jericho for relatives.

Afterwards we visited CMA missionaries George and Lola Breaden in Lebanon. Middle-eastern food, the ruins of Balbec, a church in Damasus, Syria. And then on to Rome, where Mom wanted to rest more.

"I'm getting tired from all the walking, Gordon," Mom declared. Danny and David, 7 and 5 years old were good travelers but they needed naps. So Dad, Ro and I toured the Vatican and the Coliseum, and later we all watched history replayed with sound and lights in the old Roman ruins.

"We're so blessed, Dad. Here I get to actually see places I've studied about! I love Rome, and this old hotel we're staying in, with the delicious croissant and strong coffee each morning. This is what we should always have for breakfast."

"It is wonderful, Marlene, that you and Ro get to see Israel and Europe at your age. Many never come, or only sightsee when they're much older."

In Paris we rode up the Eiffel Tower, toured the Louvre, floated down the Seine in an open cruise boat. A couple sitting across from us were kissing passionately. Romaine and I watched at length. They paused and smiled at us, then continued. "They'll have sore lips," Romaine joked.

That night we walked around the artistic Montmartre quarter, where a young hippie was strumming a guitar on the steps of the big white church. "How special" I thought. "I want to come back here someday."

Arriving in London, we stayed only one night. We had decided as a family we would trade in our air tickets for a cruise across the Atlantic. The ship with its lavish dining rooms, large pools, and movie theater was so opulent. A whole different world. My new red and white batik dress sewn at a tailor shop in Dalat seemed out of date already among the fashion conscious passengers. When we docked in New York City I would need to observe and absorb a whole fresh culture.

ONE YEAR TO ADJUST

I was looking forward to visiting Grandma and Grandpa Larson in their square green house in Jamestown, New York. Only Grandma was now upstairs in bed, slowly dying of throat cancer. It had travelled to her eyes and she was blind now, and so precious. "How are you, Marlene?"

"I'm good, Grandma. It's so good to see you again. We've been praying for you." There were long silences. At 16 I didn't know how to relate well. I wish I had been eloquent with love, details of my life, appreciation for her sacrifice of us to missions. But almost speechless I gazed at the swollen, weeping mass that was once an eye, and just held her hand.

Dad spent time with her, and also with Grandpa. She died a few weeks later, and after the funeral I remember feeling that something was missing. What was it? It was something spiritual—the climate over us had changed. After awhile I decided it must be that her prayers for us were missing. Grandma was an intercessor, and the extra covering grace she had prayed daily over us was now gone.

Before we settled back in Livonia, Michigan Dad was assigned by the CMA to be the mission speaker at a kids' camp north of Toronto, Canada. Since he would be working on his PhD in Ann Arbor all year, he could this way fulfill his mission speaking requirements.

Our family settled into housing at the larger Glen Rocks Family Camp, while Dad ministered at Camp Witmoc next door in the evenings. While eating Glen Rocks family meals, swimming at the lake, and attending evening services we met teenaged staff workers. Romaine and I made friends with them, and one decided to nickname me Marti. "It's shorter, easier to say," she explained. I liked it. Then one of the most popular boys took an interest in me—Mike Chambers. He was dark haired with clear brown eyes, outgoing, and wanted to be a missionary doctor. And he liked me!

My emotional life was jolted. My low self-esteem began to lift, to soar. I could hardly eat. The last three weeks of Dad's assignment Ro and I washed dishes at the smaller Camp Witmoc. Stacks of dirty dishes! But I tried to make the evening services at Glen Rocks…and Mike and I would talk. He gave me devotional books…he wanted us to memorize scripture together. He kissed me…my life brimmed with happiness.

We said goodbye, promising to write.

Romaine and I rode the bus together to Bentley High School from our new rambler home that was set on a long street in front of thick woods. Dan and Dave rode a different bus.

Ro was a sophomore, I was a senior. It was our last year as a whole family together and a beginning of life for me in America.

We were both excited. Mom had bought new clothes for us that summer of 1964, and we were trying to be stylish, to fit in. Dad took a picture of us putting on makeup in front of the mirror one morning. I had short curly blond hair…Ro's was a little longer. My red winter coat, thick scarf, and tall boots made me feel dashing.

Bentley had 2400 students, with 700 in their senior year. An enormous change from Dalat School, but I was eager, ready to be immersed in a new culture. Having read Mom's monthly Ladies Home Journal in the

Ilaga, I was going to experience some of this Western culture for myself. And I would introduce myself as Marti.

The first day was the hardest--finding the right classrooms amid the packed hallways, sitting at lunch trying not to feel alone. I took marching band and made third chair in clarinet, a place where I made friends. Jean played clarinet also, a Christian, also a senior…we began to eat lunch together.

The classes were not hard—Dalat had been much steeper academically. But it took me awhile to get a handle on social life. I observed there were two main subcultures at Bentley: the Greasers and the Frats. Greasers dressed mostly in black and subtly rejected the status quo. Guys in tight jeans, slicked hair, girls with high teased hair, and eyes thick with mascara. The Frats looked clean cut, collegiate—as if they were preparing for the sororities and fraternities they would someday fit into. They sat more toward the front of the class and often made better grades.

I was definitely more of a frat, but socially very tentative. A boy behind me in algebra sniffed the air and nudged me. "What perfume do you wear?"

"White Shoulders," I answered.

"Hmmmm. Do you party?"

I reflected. "What does 'party' mean?"

"Hang out. Drink a little."

"Well no, not really."

"Okay."

Applying at Crowley's Department Store down the road from us, I began working 16-20 hours a week in the junior high clothes department. My styles improved as I spent wages on my wardrobe.

One tall girl in my department—Lisa—seemed very mature and knowledgeable about clothes, giving ideas for advertising them to our supervisor. I was impressed. She was my age, engaged to be married after graduation. I tried to imagine her outlook on life. I had nurses' training and college ahead of me. Why did she want to limit her future potential? Did she just expect to have children and stay working at Crowleys all her life? Could she be a supervisor there without a college degree?

It seemed so confining. Such a small circumference. In my view there were mountains to climb, and Lisa was settling for a plot on the plains.

I began to think of college—there were two that offered a B.S. in Missions for Nurses. I could take two years of Bible college with three years in nursing at either institution—in Rochester, New York, or St. Paul, Minnesota.

But what if I did something more fun—like become a flight attendant? Through the years of flying I had observed these attendants with interest. They led exciting lives flying from place to place, and always looked glamorous. I prayed about it for awhile, and the Lord spoke to me. "I called you to be a missionary nurse. Remember that."

"Yes, Lord."

I applied to both schools and prayed that the right one would accept me first. St Paul Bible's registrar wrote back a welcome, and I accepted. It happened to be the Bible school that my Grandpa Larson had attended one semester, when he and Grandma had lived in Minnesota.

On graduation day from Bentley High parents lined the bleachers in the hot sun while their offspring trooped slowly through the line. Two people took turns reading the 700 names. Dad, linguistically observant, phonetically marked the cadence of each one on paper, staving off boredom. The family cheered as Marlene Larson took her diploma.

I wanted to work for two months as staff at Glen Rocks Bible Camp in Canada. Mom and Dad protested. "This is our last summer together, Marlene. We can have family times…go shopping for college clothes together," Mom said. But I was adamant. Knowing the family was leaving, I had begun to emotionally detach myself. I would defer my frequent teenage arguments with Mom this way, and gain more independence.

And I did have fun at Glen Rocks. Mike wasn't staffing that summer, but I dated a tall guy named Fred for awhile, and we started going together. And there were powerful sermons each night at chapel, especially when Dr. Bernard King taught one week, covering the book of

Jude. But when I returned Mom and Dad were packing up, and there was little spare time to enjoy one another.

Aunt Christine and Uncle Maxey took us to the airport…and it was there I began to realize my tremendous loss. Four years—I wouldn't see them for four years! Mom was preoccupied with details of hand luggage as we hurried down the airport concourse, and keeping track of Danny and David.

"Mom—aren't you going to say goodbye to me?"

"Oh, Marlene, of course I am!" She became tearful and hugged me. Dad bear-hugged me, and I kissed Ro, Dan and Dave goodbye. They boarded the plane and Aunt Christine stood with me a long time as it taxied down the runway and finally soared off.

Four years.

I had left home.

I was supposed to be grown up.

CRISIS IN THE CALL

THE CASTLE

The large red brick building which housed St. Paul Bible College was both friendly and forbidding. The cold drizzly day, the tall turrets, the high-ceilinged reception room and creaky stairs were cold and austere. But the staff were warm, my roommate engaging, our room small and cozy. I settled into a routine of English, history, and Bible classes. And I made friends over lunch in the cafeteria.

Mr. Tewinkel's history class was enlightening, Dr. Richardson's theology class faith-building. But it was Dr. Mason's New Testament class that enthralled me. He illumined the historical background and hidden details of a Bible narrative to made it live afresh. Years later as I read scripture I would remember his penetrating comments. "I would love to teach like that," I sighed to myself. "His instruction affects people so deeply, so well."

The president Dr. Hardwick once greeted me by name in the hallway. I was stunned. Someone later told me that he memorized all of the 400 plus students by name. He probably prayed for us by name also.

I kept looking in my mailbox for letters. Mom and Dad wrote faithfully, weekly. And I wrote back. But I was eager for letters from my tall Fred...and when he actually broke off the relationship I was devastated. I was desperate for family and friendship closeness. Mom and Dad were halfway around the world, and now there was no connection with Fred. The Kentucky and New York relatives were so far away, and I didn't feel close to anyone to telephone, to pour out my heart.

"Lord, please let the next man I go with be the one I will marry," I prayed. "I just don't want to be hurt anymore. Or waste time."

Grandpa Larson was paying most of my room, board, and tuition. I was very grateful, writing to thank him after each check he sent. And the allowance I received from the CMA I put toward my school fees. That meant I needed to find a part time job for spending money. Scouting around, I interviewed for a 20 hour a week job at a fudge booth in a department store.

Chapel was a welcome break in our morning classes. We met in a large medieval room with tall organ pipes and a balcony overlooking the platform with rows of seating below. Worship, inspiring speakers, announcements. Leaning down to grab my books at the end of chapel one morning I bumped heads with a brown haired freshman sitting next to me. He was reaching for his books too. We laughed, rubbing our foreheads. "Hi, I'm Marti Larson," I said.

"Well hello, I'm Zachary Smith. Nice to meet you!"

He began to drop in at my fudge booth at work, and make small talk.

Christmas was coming! I rode a Greyhound bus long hours to Buffalo, New York to spend a snowy Christmas with Uncle Dewey, Aunt Petey, and my cousins Sherrie, Cindy and John. The holiday was special, but not the same as being with Mom and Dad and the family among the Danis. Riding back to Minnesota I was sober, thoughtful.

Second semester classes started and Zachary and I began sitting together in class, eating together in the cafeteria. He was originally from St. Paul, Minnesota, but now from Scottsdale, Arizona where his parents had moved for his mother's health. He was an only child, and had started at ASU fall semester, but had no peace in his heart to stay there. "Mom and Dad suggested this college--where Mom had attended years ago--and after prayer we felt this was the right choice. So I drove here in my Barracuda and started school late."

"I love your car!" I exclaimed. It was a white sports car, with a long hatchback.

Zach laughed. "It gets me around!" He was muscular, of medium height, with blue eyes and an aristocratic nose. He had an easy laugh, a good sense of humor. Dr. Gates the philosophy professor with cerebral palsy loved to have Zach wheel him and assist him at lunch.

I had quit my job some weeks earlier, and Zach suggested I might work at a small hospital nearby where he had found a part time job. I applied and soon found myself working in admissions afternoons and evenings, taking new patients to their rooms. I was thrilled to be in a hospital! "Someday I'll be a nurse, actually working with patients," I thought. "And someday I'll be in Irian Jaya, working among a tribe."

As we dated, Zach and I talked about my call to missions. He was majoring in history, but had a desire to help people, to reach them with the Gospel. He decided to switch his major to mission work. We got to know Bill Conley, a former missionary to Indonesia, who now taught missions classes. He and his wife had all the MKs over for a meal in their beautiful home. I was so grateful. Here was a couple I could relate to who understood my world. They had worked among the Dyacks in Borneo.

I found three other freshmen also working toward a B.S. in Missions for Nurses. We all applied to Swedish Hospital School of Nursing. After three years we would have nursing diplomas, then could finish our last year of Bible school.

As summer break approached I prayed for direction. "Lord, please guide me. Open the right door for work, among friends or family." I considered different options...staying in St. Paul, or going to Kentucky, or New York.

Soon afterwards a new friend Dawn Wheelock from Phoenix, Arizona made me an offer. "Why don't you come home with me? My folks would like to have you—I'll ask them. You can find work for the summer and also be near Zach."

DESERT LIGHTNING

And so it worked out. I flew to Phoenix, and Zach and his parents met me at the airport—he had driven there a few days earlier. We were all delighted. Evey Smith was small, fragile and pretty, walking awkwardly because of the muscular dystrophy she struggled with. Outgoing and enthusiastic, she made everything special, looking at the bright side of life. Zach's dad Bob was tall and genial, a World War II veteran who had survived concentration camp. He was quieter, an accountant (who ran his business from his home) and made life run smoothly. I loved them both.

Zach hugged me closely, and we drove to meet the Wheelocks, where I would stay for the summer. Chuck and Doris settled me into their comfortable ranch home that had a view of Camelback Mountain. Dawn and I shared a room, she gave me clothes…I was cared for, loved. God was so faithful!

The hot weeks slid into months of blazing Arizona summer. Mrs. Smith drove me around till I found a job at Gigi's, waitressing. The culture of the servers amazed me. There was one girl not much older than me who was already getting divorced. She argued loudly on the phone with her almost-ex-husband. Most of my peers were living independently, juggling work and boyfriends. I was still adapting to American culture.

On Sundays I attended the large Baptist church with the Smiths, and slowly acquainted myself with Zach's thriving college group. The leaders were a young couple with children who somehow found time to host a variety of exciting activities for us all. I begged Isabel my boss to reschedule me so I could attend some of them. We met for bowling, parties in homes, trips to the mountains. One Saturday our group went to Sliding Rock, near Sedona. We picnicked, splashed, rested, and finally headed in a caravan back to Phoenix.

Along the way, descending into the hot desert Zach and I stopped to watch lightning play in the distance. The sky was dark and windy. Mountains of purple and gray clouds swelled, rumbled, as long jags of flashing light lit the whole scrubbed terrain. It was glorious! Zach and I laid on the car hood for a long time watching the play of light and darkness, the roar of war in the heavens. If this was so beautiful and awesome, what must God's throne and the banks of Heaven look like? Raindrops began pelting down, so hurrying inside his white car we paused for a long kiss…then slowly continued our descent into hazy, hot Phoenix.

Zach and I spent many evenings together that summer, and had enjoyable times time with his parents. Quiet and peaceable, they had no lively penetrating discussions over issues like my family. They were validating. Dad Noll did pray sincere long prayers over the meals, but I don't remember them ever having family devotions.

When summer ended, the Smiths drove Zach and me back to Minnesota, so for the first time I saw the Grand Canyon, Yellowstone Park, the Tetons. Astonishing beauty. We met more of Zach's relatives in South Dakota, and finally I was dropped off at Swedish Hospital in Minneapolis. I hugged the Smiths tearfully goodbye--they were like family already. Zach would continue at St. Paul Bible College across town, and I would live in downtown Minneapolis.

CRISP UNIFORMS

The student nurses' dorm was an ancient red brick building that had housed the original Swedish Hospital. The newer buildings were across the street—eight storied, tan colored. The whole complex is now Metropolitan Medical Center.

There were over 60 nursing students in my class, all female, largely from the upper Midwest. Our orientation was led by white haired Miss Linnerooth who was strict but kind. "You're like budding roses, and good disciplined habits will help you bloom well." Some girls snickered a little, others smiled thoughtfully.

As the weeks passed I tried to fit in, to adjust once again in a new subculture. Most of my classmates were living away from home for the first time. Not only was I a year older than many of them, but I'd lived away from home since 6th grade (except for my senior year). And after adjusting to one year in an American high school, and one year in a small Bible college I was weary of adapting. I missed Mom and Dad and my siblings. I missed being with Zach. I was in downtown Minneapolis, trying to fit in with an all-girl student body that seemed two-dimensional--it even felt like a modern nunnery of sorts.

Also, these girls only knew America. I was very Dani in my heart, but I knew that telling too many stories of tribal life might make me seem extreme and different to them. So I slowly made a few good friends, but didn't immerse myself fully into the student body life.

On a deeper level, however I felt fulfilled, since nursing school was key in walking out God's call on my life. At long last, I was going to live the dream of caring for the sick, delivering babies, binding up wounds. Eventually I would return overseas to reach a tribe, share the gospel. So I tried to take the long view, to plunge into my studies with diligence. I liked our crisp uniforms—white collared, blue pin-striped, with a starched white pinafore.

Our clinicals were practical and basic: learning to take blood pressures, make a hospital bed, give backrubs, chart. Eventually we gave injections, inserted Foleys, started IV's. I found that the abstract bookwork was easier for me than the practical hands on work—and I was surprised.

I continued to date Zach on weekends, and we went to church together. We often visited his grandparents in St. Paul, a retired pastor couple who became like family. Their modest, conservative home was a haven. But there was an emptiness in me, a need for closeness, and I looked to Zach to fill it. Even a missed evening phone call from him made me uneasy and restless.

As I continued to write my parents faithfully, one time I shared my loneliness and struggle. Mom wrote back their concern, and that my father had even wept over my pain--and I had hardly ever seen my dad cry. By that time my crisis had passed, so I decided then that I couldn't share my whole heart in letters. It was unfair to my parents. But I felt more isolated then, and I leaned on Zach more. And we got too emotionally and physically close, with heavy petting, which made me feel guilty. I did confess to the Lord, and continued to seek Him.

Romaine arrived in the States after my first year, slightly taller than me now, with long golden hair. She was cheerful, had enjoyed her years at Dalat. And she would be at St. Paul Bible, where Zach was. So she and Zach attended my capping ceremony—a big milestone back when nurses wore caps! I glowed with joy and pride over my winged glory, my long blond hair tucked up into it. If only Mom and Dad could have been there!

A few of our nursing classes were at nearby McAllister College, so we walked to the campus through open fields. Microbiology was rather pedantic, but anthropology was a joy--I loved the study of other cultures. Our instructor Mr. Habib, a swarthy Indian from Bombay, took an interest in me. He played some of my father's videos of the Ilaga Valley in our class after I showed them to him.

"You don't have to take the final, Marti," he confided to me later. "You already know about all this multiculturalism."

RAINBOW FIRE

Looking back, I realize what large decisions I was making during this time in life--confirmation of life calling, whom I should marry, what stream of the body of Christ I would flow in. Decisions made at the age of 21 affected the direction of my whole life.

The following summer Zach joined a mission trip to Ecuador where he lived among tribal people, helping with a building project. I missed him desperately, but was glad for the grassroots experience he was having. I eagerly looked for letters as I lived in the dorm during our five week summer break. I continued working part time in nursing, as first year students could make a fair wage.

But I wasn't excited about hospital nursing. I came to dread those summer shifts. Finally I asked God whether I should continue nurses training. "Lord, I want to do your will. But I don't enjoy taking care of people in a hospital. Is this really your purpose for me? Will I feel satisfied ministering medically among a tribe for the rest of my life? Is this the best way you can use me?"

In time I had peace to continue. I was in God's will....this was the training He had for me now.

After Ecuador Zach flew to Alaska to help in a building project with Alaska Village Missions. He stayed on and later worked in salmon fishing for a couple weeks, earning good wages. When he came back after visiting his parents in Arizona, our reunion was sweet. "I missed you so much," I whispered as he hugged me tight.

He proposed that fall and together we looked at diamonds in downtown Minneapolis. We had a ring designed with a curve where the diamond would be set. One evening after an elegant dinner at La Brassiere Restaurant he slipped the ring on my finger and kissed me. "I love you so much," he said. His blue eyes were tender. "We'll have our whole lives together."

"No more long months apart," I agreed.

Back at the dorm my friend Cyndie Rydholm rejoiced with me, laughing. Later that night I held my ring up to the light and watched its flashing rainbow fire. "Thank you, Lord, thank you."

Zach had written my parents and asked for my hand….they had given permission. We planned to be married in a year and a half, after I graduated and they were home on furlough.

The following summer I was alone again, making more money as a student nurse, but desperate for closeness and family. Zach was in Phoenix with his parents, and most classmates were home with families. I reached out to my friend Cyndie, who was living in the dorm that summer also. We sometimes prayed together, and I sensed she had more spiritual strength than I did. Cyndie came from a Pentecostal background, and one evening she invited me to a prayer meeting at North Central Bible College. I went with her, hungry for more of God.

I remembered back to my senior year in Michigan when Dad and I had once attended a Catholic charismatic service. Nuns and priests and others were worshipping, singing in the Spirit. God's presence was so strong. I had wanted to press into what they had, but didn't know how.

So at the meeting I asked for prayer. I wanted the filling, the baptism in the Holy Spirit. People laid hands on my shoulders and prayed. I confessed sin, any unforgiveness, any dealing with the occult in my life. (I had read horoscopes, played with a ouji board a few times.) They prayed, I prayed. I wanted all I could get from God!

Nothing seemed to change. I did not feel anything or speak in tongues as some did when touched by the Holy Spirit. The leader encouraged me, "Sometimes this will happen when you're alone, and not self-conscious. But there is choice to receiving in faith. It's like Peter getting out of the boat when he wanted to walk to Jesus, on the water. He had to swing his legs out and walk. So just open your mouth and speak."

I thanked him, and Cyndie and I walked home. Later alone in my pink-curtained bedroom I prayed again. "Alright, Jesus. I asked you for the baptism in the Holy Spirit, and you promised to give Him. So I receive." And I opened my mouth, began speaking in slow syllables. I realized I was saying "All el u ia" very slowly. And then the prayer language came. A slow rushing of unknown words, like a flowing river. And I felt very peaceful, full of joy. I was full—of Him!

I rushed down to Cyndie's room to give her the good news. "He answered! I'm speaking in tongues!" She hugged me, and we prayed in the Spirit together for awhile, and then I went to bed.

This peace and joy filled me for days and weeks as I continued to seek the Lord. But slowly it tapered off. Not realizing how much I needed fellowship and worship to keep momentum and fullness in God, I slowed down. And had less power to obey wholeheartedly.

CHRISTMAS TREES AND CANDLES

When Zach returned for fall semester we were together most weekend days. Campfires by the Mississippi River, walks in Minnehaha Park by the statue of Hiawatha and Minnehaha, a hike at Taylor Falls. We attended Rosedale Alliance Church on Sundays, enjoying Rev. Hall's sincere preaching and pastoral concern for us.

This fall of my senior year I also had one family member near me. Romaine had decided to become a nurse also, so she was a freshman in a nearby dorm at Swedish Hospital. We each had long, blond hair with bangs and wore the same style of glasses. We looked so much alike that for a few weeks when we were on the same hospital floor for clinicals one nursing instructor mixed us up. "Oh—I thought you were Romaine," she apologized, laughing.

By this fall Zach and I had been dating for almost three years. We were close emotionally, spiritually, and too close physically, though we didn't actually commit fornication. We would pray together, confessing sin, but the failure was repetitive. How could we overcome this? Should we get married sooner than next summer? Mom and Dad would miss the wedding...that would be so sad. For me and for them. I was their oldest...it would be the first family wedding.

We considered, prayed, communicated with our parents, and finally set the date at Dec.19, before Christmas. I knew Mom and Dad were disappointed about this decision, but didn't realize the deep cost to them, and eventually to me.

Looking for bridal dresses...I found a beautiful ivory gown on sale, with a princess style waist and longer train. Romaine liked it--I was so excited as I carried it back to the dorm. The bridesmaids would wear cranberry red velvet dresses, with white fur muffs. The wedding would be elegant!

Dad and Mom Noll helped in decorating Rosedale Church. Three Christmas trees on each side of the altar with glowing red balls, and lighted candles on the altar rails in front.

Snow had begun to fall the evening before the wedding. Big thick flakes that drifted and piled high. So of the 300 invited, only around 100 could make it. Dr. Conley the missionary from Indonesia walked me down the aisle to Zach who looked so handsome in his tuxedo, brown hair freshly cut. Francis Assisi's song was sung "Let me be an Instrument of Thy Peace," and at the end "So send I you, to labor unrewarded..." A mission song of commitment. Zach and I said our vows, looking into one another's eyes, as Rev. Hall officiated.

I was so happy.

But I missed Mom and Dad.

From my side of the family there was only Romaine, standing up front, smiling at me.

After the reception we greeted guests and celebrated with cake until most had driven away through the snowdrifts. Then we stepped lightly through the powdered sugar sidewalk to Zach's car. "We're really married!" he exclaimed.

"I can hardly take it in," I laughed. "A dream come true."

TWO ROOMED NEST

Zach and I drove north to honeymoon a few days at a resort on Big Sandy Lake. The snowstorm had made a winter wonderland...after sleeping in blissfully we trudged through drifts and fir trees by the frozen lake. Later we sat by a roaring fire and ate delicious meals in the rustic dining room.

We made it back to St. Paul in time to spend Christmas with family, then drove to Phoenix where Dan's parents hosted a big reception at their church. I wore a silver sparkly dress trimmed with fur, and felt so special.

More gifts, more great food, more love. We drove back to Minnesota laden with boxes of blankets, towels, dishes, silverware, and a big box of cookies and candy—Mom was a consummate artist in baking Christmas cookies.

We set up housekeeping in a two roomed apartment up the stairs on 8th street. It was near Elliot Park, across from a mission for homeless people where we had found cheap rent. Grandma and Grandpa helped us clean and paint...even put fresh linoleum on the old kitchen countertop.

I hung curtains, arranged our few pieces of furniture, with a wall divider to separate the tiny living room space from the bedroom. Zach had refinished his grandmother's old hope chest, so that became a small couch in the living room, across from which sat a pair of solid oak chairs, new blue brocade cushions on them. A donated bookshelf was filled, and a few pictures artfully hung. On the other side of the divider was the bed and dresser—no room for more. Aunt Inez's thick cream colored bedspread gave the space an air of distinction.

The kitchen was the second room, with a bathroom attached. After putting our new dishes and pots and pans away in the cupboards, and covering the little kitchen table with a dark green cloth, our first home was cozy. I celebrated by having Miss Linnerooth over for dinner one night.

During my last year I enjoyed the obstetric and surgery rotations. Each delivery of a tiny human was an enormous miracle to witness. And surgery was a field electric to me--precise in preparation, procedure, closure. A sterile field with ingenious tools to dissect, excise, suture, staple. I loved viewing the insides of people. How amazing was the God-designed body where organs fit together, energized by warm blood.

One day I was scrubbed and gloved to assist with an abdominal surgery on a very large patient. At a certain point another tech and I were told to pull on large deavers to help widen the surgeons' view. My deaver curled over the thick layer of abdominal fat, and I pulled hard.

"Harder!"

The tech and I pulled opposite ways, opening the abdomen as far as we could. I felt sorry for the surgeon, sorry for the patient. He would be in so much pain after waking! Viewing all the inches of white fat I determined to watch my weight carefully. Heavy people struggled in so many ways.

As June and graduation approached I began studying for state boards. We had to pass minimum state scores in each area of nursing before we could be hired. Zach studied his classes, and we each worked part time.

Mom and Dad, Danny and David flew from Irian Jaya just in time for my graduation. Dan was 13, tall and articulate, Dave 11—quieter, husky with playing sports. Dad had a beard like an Amish preacher, all around his chin, and still looked handsome. Mom was lively, happy, her honey colored hair curled.

Everyone loved Zach's easy going humor…they met the Smiths who had come to town, and Grandma and Grandpa Hofer. We were one big family at my graduation, my loved ones beaming as I received the diploma. The circle of my life was complete that night.

MOTORCYCLING TO ALASKA

Zach and I each had another year of Bible college before graduation—but Zach was ready for a break. "Why don't we take a semester off and help out at Alaska Village Missions in Homer," he suggested. "I could do some building for them, and you could find some nursing work nearby."

I liked the idea. "Say--why don't we go up on a big motorcycle," I suggested. "We could sell your truck and buy a Harley!" We loved motorcycles and this would be an adventure indeed.

"Well, Lee Downey and Wes Syverson and some other guys are thinking of cycling up to Anchorage to work for the summer…maybe we could join them," Zach mused.

So, after more discussion and prayer we did just that. We sold the truck, bought a 1200cc full dress Harley, and stored our belongings in Grandma and Grandpa Hofer's basement. Mom and Dad and the family were moving to Nyack, New York for a semester, where Dad would teach cultural anthropology to future CMA mission workers.

After they left Zach and I stayed with Grandma and Grandpa, preparing for the trip. We had purchased black leather jackets and white helmets....Dan painted patriotic blue and red ribbons on his, and daisies on mine. We were set.

On a fine July day we loaded up in their front yard, four big cycles laden with camping gear, food, and clothes. Lee, Wes, Tom, Zach, and I were excited. Grandma and Grandpa were dubious but accepting. We prayed together for a safe journey, and roared off.

Soon after, at a stoplight I got an exhaust burn on my inner leg. Unbelievable—we had barely started! A pharmacist nearby helped with ointment and a bandage, and each day afterwards I changed the dressing till the burn healed.

West, farther west we chugged, all day through South Dakota in uncommon heat, getting sunburnt. It turned out to indeed be a day of extremes. Our Harley had three blowouts on the rear tire. Each time Zach patched and filled the tire with air, but got more nervous in driving. We would wobble and nearly hurtle off the road! After the third tire repair the weather drastically changed. Strong wind nearly pressed us over, black banks of clouds marched across the sky...then the atmosphere looked faintly green, grew very quiet.

When we sighted a small tunnel of cloud farther west we stopped by the side of the road. "Look," Lee said. "There's a culvert over there if the tornado comes too close." We watched, fascinated as the spiral shaped tunnel danced over the fields, coming closer, north of us.

It touched down in a farmyard about a mile away and moved farther east.

And then the wind blew! So strong I thought it might push our cycles over. A few trucks and cars were parked by the side of the road, so we ran to some of them for cover. Zach and I and Lee were welcomed into a big rig by a trucker, huddling till the storm passed. As the rain lessened we thanked him profusely.

"Don't mention it," he said, smiling.

That night we decided to pay for rooms rather than camp. We were exhausted. Coming upon an old hotel the five of us shared two rooms, hauling up our bags. Some of my pancake mix had spilled through a duffel bag, and I cleaned it up. "Why did we bring so much food?" I thought to myself. I climbed into bed next to Zach, grateful to be warm and safe.

"This is quite an adventure, Zachary."

"Yes," he murmured sleepily. "We won't forget this!"

We were about three weeks on the road, mostly camping out at night. Some mornings we had a time of prayer before starting. Wes and Lee were interested in pastoring, Zach and I in mission work. Tom was quiet, sincere in his faith, growing. There were pastor friends along the way--so one night we stayed with them—on July 21, 1969 when the astronauts walked on the moon. We watched history happen on the black and white TV as Neil Armstrong made his giant step for humanity on the moon's face! And we were living our own history cycling across the northwest.

Finally, saddle sore and weary we camped in a park near Prince Rupert, on the Pacific coast of Canada. It happened to be the weekend, when local whites and Indians were celebrating on the town. The five of us wandered among them, observing the raucous flavor, eventually wolfing down a good meal and collapsing in our tents. The next day we booked passages on a ferry heading up the Pacific coast. We were cutting out 1,000 miles of dirt road by taking the ferry.

After boarding we watched the magnificent coastline scenery, passing Ketchikan, Wrangell, and stopping in Juneau for a few hours. We debarked on a cold, misty afternoon with other cars at Haines, and headed up the Alcan Highway. Four hundred miles of dirt road before we hit pavement. Mud and mist and high meadows. Desolate, except for wildlife. I huddled behind Zach, trying to stay warm. Tom's cycle sputtered and broke down near a highway maintenance station, and the men worked with it, finally deciding it would have to be shipped to a motorcycle shop. Having arranged for that with the maintenance crew, John rode behind Lee and we pushed forward through the fog.

Cold and bone-weary I remember numbly watching a vehicle coming toward us on the muddy road thinking, "Why didn't we drive to Alaska in a car, like most people?" When we finally reached Anchorage, another pastor couple took the five of us into their basement bedrooms. Sleeping well for a few nights I was restored.

But Homer was our destination, so hugging Wes, Lee, and Tom goodbye we chugged south on the Kenai Peninsula to Homer. A frontier town set on a hillside, it overlooked Kachemak Bay with a spit of land protruding into it, and with mountains and a glacier beyond. A picturesque landscape.

Ray and Petra Arno welcomed us into their home. We stayed with them around ten days, attended their church, and then moved into empty Bible school housing outside of town on a hill.

Unpacking our few belongings in the tiny furnished duplex, I taped large watercolor pictures to the wall above the sofa, making it homey. Zach began helping other carpenters build, and I borrowed an old van and looked for work. The local hospital couldn't use me as a nurse because my state board scores hadn't been issued, and I couldn't apply for a nursing license. But there was a crab cannery at the end of the long spit, and yes, they would hire me! And so with tall rubber boots and a warm jacket, one morning I started for work.

QUONSET HUT IN THE ALEUTIANS

The culture of this Alaskan crab cannery was singular. Russian immigrant women worked here, their hair covered in babushka scarves. They spoke little English. There were frontier hippie people (rather nomadic, like me), Aleuts, regular Alaskan Indians, and white settlers. As the large wire containers of king crab were lifted into the warehouse, they were plunged into boiling water. After being cooked the legs were torn off, blown free of white meat with pressurized water, and further down the conveyer line I sorted white from red meat with other workers.

We were allowed to eat as much crab as we wanted…but after a few days I couldn't eat it anymore. It was cold, wet work, so I was glad to sit at lunch resting my legs, eat my sandwich, and sip coffee with other workers.

I prayed for these people. Many seemed emotionally weary, somewhat hardened, bruised from the storms of life. In time a couple of women from the mission joined me, as they needed extra income also. I was grateful for this work—we had almost depleted our savings from the long trip north.

The mission team met from time to time, and Ray shared that he planned a trip to Port Heiden, a small village on the Aleutian Peninsula. He wanted to build a church with a tiny apartment attached where mission workers could stay. As more Aleuts accepted the Lord some could be trained in the Bible school in Homer to minister to their own tribe. In a few weeks he would fly builders down to work on the project.

Zach was interested...I was piqued also. What would the remote village be like? The Aleutian Islands were windswept and desolate, we heard. The tribe made most of their living from seal trade.

Weeks rolled by as Zach and others built a new duplex dorm on the mission hill. I continued to sort crab and get to know the workers. We had a couple of the men from the cannery over for a rabbit stew dinner one night. Somehow the liquid boiled away, so we ate burnt rabbit! We joked, told stories, shared the gospel, and listened to their tales of laboring in the frozen oil fields further north.

Ray Arno made preparations for the three week expedition to Port Heiden, and Zach and I offered to go, packing clothes and sleeping bags. I had quit work and was to be the chief cook and dishwasher for the team of five. We flew near snowcapped peaks, south across blue ocean as Ray searched for landmarks among the islands. After an hour or so we landed and bounced down on hard packed beach.

Climbing out I was amazed at the landscape. Terns and ptarmigans wheeled through the pale blue sky, dark waves washed tawny sand, wind blew strong over flat, scrubby land. No trees...no trees at all! Just a few scattered white painted houses in the distance, some curved quonset huts, and a small building that housed the generator. It would be started up before dark each night, so the village could have electricity.

Ray greeted some village men, and we all dragged boxes and bags into an empty quonset. There were cots in the large room, a small refrigerator, a two-burner cooktop stove, a table with chairs. And an outhouse!

For three weeks I cooked meals—lunch and dinner, that is. For breakfast the men fended for themselves and I got up to dress for the day after they left. Ray flew back and forth a couple of times from Homer with lumber and supplies. That particular evening we had a gathering of the village in the schoolhouse. We sang worship songs, heard a Bible story geared for the numerous children, and ended with cookies and candy.

I met the village schoolteacher and chatted with her. "You must be really dedicated, to live in this isolated village for so long, teaching all the grades together in one room!" I exclaimed.

"Well, yes, I care for the children, or I wouldn't be here. If they can have a good education it can make a lot of difference. Sometimes their home life is not so good." I squeezed her hand as we parted, and her lined face lit with a smile.

In the long afternoons I visited some of the homes, and especially made friends with Jenny, an Aleut mom in her 30's. We chatted over coffee.

"It must be lonely in the long winters here, huh?"

"Yes, especially when Jeff is gone for weeks working in Anchorage. And sometimes the people here drink a lot—that's hard on their kids. I'm not a drinker. I want our kids to grow up strong."

"That's great, Jenny. So, do you read the Bible when you get lonely? Are you a Christian, yourself?"

"Well, sort of. I gave my life to God a long time ago. I don't read the Bible that much."

I kept visiting, our friendship grew. One day Jenny prayed with me, giving her life back to God. I encouraged her to teach her kids Bible stories, to pray with them.

Occasionally Zach and I walked the long beaches, picking up seashells and green glass fishing bobbers. Gulls wheeled overhead and screeched, the wind blew incessantly. Waves washing, wind whirling across grasses. The land was grand and bare, scoured clean by the weather.

At night sharing the cot with Dan, I listened to the wind and the distant chug of the generator. Soothing, but it could be lonely, unless God had planted you here. His Presence would fill the emptiness, press in meaning.

Before we left, early one morning we were jolted by knocks at the door. "Is there a nurse here? We heard there was one. A guy at the old radar base down the road shot himself in the leg—we think he was drinking."

Zach and I jounced down the dirt road to the World War II military outpost. The middle aged man was in pain, his calf muscle pulled away from the bone, hanging loose. I was shaky…what could I do? They had some first aid supplies, and had called for a military plane.

I closed the gaping wound as best I could with clean cloth, and took the man's blood pressure and pulse. They were stable. "Do you have any medicine for pain?"

"We have Darvon here, and aspirin."

The man swallowed the Darvon, and I kept taking his vitals every fifteen minutes. He was more sober now. We prayed with him…and when we heard the drone of the plane at daylight, I was so relieved. I reported to the doctor the man's vitals and the plane took off.

"I don't like emergencies like that," I told Zach. I've only worked in a hospital setting—not on my own!

In a couple of days we flew back to Homer with Ray. The church was nearly finished…we were the first load home. Taking off on the beach, I gazed out the window. Caribou grazed in herds among the island grasses. Climbing higher, looking north I could see white peaked mountains—ranges of them. Petra must have a lot of faith to have Ray fly back and forth so much. "Did she worry?" I wondered. If their lives were God's, all was on the altar. They were living sacrifices poured out.

We were heading back to the Lower 48 now that winter was coming, but it was too cold to ride by cycle. So we had the Harley shipped to Phoenix, where Zach's parents were, then said goodbye to Ray and Petra, and the others.

Catching a plane from Anchorage, we landed in Phoenix, shocked at the heat, happy to see Mom and Dad Smith. We decided to buy a truck—

we couldn't ride the motorcycle to school in the Minnesota winters. We found a white one in a car lot, with payments!

My parents were in Nyack, New York and since I hadn't been with them for so many Christmases we decided to spend the holiday there, and celebrate early in Phoenix with Zach's parents. Laden with presents from them we then drove long miles to the northeast, and celebrated again in snowy New York.

Mom and Dad, Danny and David and Romaine. How amazing to be all together by the Christmas tree after so many years. No Ilaga Danis, no pig feast, but we had each other, in a furnished missionary apartment near Nyack Bible College.

WIDENING HORIZONS

During our stay in eastern New York Zach and I got to hear Dad teach the graduate students anthropology at Nyack Seminary. My father was a good teacher, with plenty of illustrations of tribal life, and I could tell the students loved him. They even took up an offering to help with tuition for him to attend the University of Michigan in Ann Arbor the spring semester. Dad was working on his PhD in cultural anthropology.

We all loaded up a U-Haul trailer and caravanned to Ann Arbor, setting up the Christmas tree again there, in student housing. Missionaries were adjustable--they had to be, I decided. But sometimes it was hard on my mother. Each furlough that she visited her siblings' lovely homes and then lived in a rented place, I saw the longing in her for her own home. Our cherished dwelling in the Ilaga was simple and rustic--we all loved it. But someday they would retire and leave that home, and start all over again in the States.

Zach and I hugged everyone goodbye and headed back to Minnesota to continue his missions degree spring semester, and to find work for me. Then the following fall we would both attend St. Paul Bible College full time, and graduate.

I had passed state boards, with my highest scores in psych nursing, but I wanted to work in surgery, so I searched the newspaper ads. The scrubbing and gowning of surgery, the draping, incising, dissecting, suturing...the flick of instruments into the surgeon's gloved palm, the pull of long strands of suture--I loved it all. I wanted to practice, be proficient. And I was hired at small Samaritan Hospital in St. Paul that served many retired railroad workers.

We found an upstairs furnished apartment in an older home a few blocks from the hospital. I unpacked and made it cozy. For one semester I worked days 7 to 3:30, trying to be efficient and fit into the surgical team. And Zach studied, wrote papers, worked part time on building projects. Friday nights we watched Sonny and Cher, Laugh-In, ate Saturday nights at Mama Rosa's in the university hippy area of Minneapolis. Life was interesting, rather fun.

Over my long blond hair I tied a bandana, and wore gold wire rimmed glasses, bell bottom jeans. As Zach grew his hair longer, he got reprimanded by someone at the Bible college. I felt badly about it--Zachary was rather indifferent.

During these days I had an inspiration. "Why don't we see if we can save money toward a summer trip to Europe? We could buy a motorcycle in London, use the Five Dollars a Day in Europe to travel cheaply, see a lot of countries. When we have kids and settle down in missions we won't be as free—but now we are!"

"That's a good idea," Zach exclaimed. "What countries would you want to travel through?"

"Well, France for sure, after England, then Italy, Switzerland, maybe to Israel?"

"Israel's a long way. We might not have time. I'd like to see Germany, where Grandma and Grandpa Hofer are from."

After thought and prayer we prepared passports, checked on flights. We could buy a 650cc Bonneville in London reasonably, so we ordered one. And we sold our bigger motorcycle in Phoenix, with Dad Smith's help. Sometime in June there was enough money to take the trip. God had provided.

Europe was incredible. Quaint English streets with tall bed and breakfast hotels lined up, the changing of the guard at Windsor Castle, the wax museum with Henry VIII's wives beside him. Trafalgar Square, with pigeons flying around the tall monument. In this summer of 1970 the movie Oliver was playing in theaters, and that afternoon the young actor himself was being filmed in the square for promotional purposes. He was running, guiding a hoop with a baton, but all of us tourists were not to be seen in the filming! Reluctantly, we moved.

Eventually we found the crowded cycle shop, run by a chubby red-cheeked man who chain-smoked cigarettes. The paperwork took hours, and finally the 650cc Bonneville was ours, and we roared down the street back to the hotel. In a day or two we decided to head toward Bath where a large rock music festival was being held. But since tickets were too expensive, we left Bath and headed southwest to Lorna Doone country between Devon and Somerset. Pushing onward, we entered rain and mist, finally reaching Tiverton and Blundell's School in late afternoon.

The place, the very place that the Lorna Doone book began! We peered through a tall iron gate at the yellowed stone buildings across wide lawns. R.D. Blackmore had described location and characters so well that the story seemed real to me. But the weather was so cold. As we cycled through the rain Zach turned his head. "I think we should head back to London now that it's raining so much. We don't want to miss the ferry reservation to France."

"You're right," I said into his ear, huddled behind him. Regretfully we turned around. "Someday, somehow we'll visit Doone Valley."

"Sure, another time."

We boarded the hydroplane ferry in sight of the chalky white cliffs of Dover, excited to see France. From Calais we rode the cycle through mist and rain to Paris. I loved the quaintness of French villages, the beauty of Paris. The Eiffel Tower, treasures of The Louvre, the rich jewel of Notre Dame, the gleaming Chartres Cathedral. How God had gifted people to create masterpiece treasures!

After a few days we headed south to Spain, determined to find hot beaches, to rest and warm up. We ended up staying north of Barcelona at a small hotel in Arenys de Mar, up the street from the beach. I liked how the Spanish families would stroll up and down the boulevard at sunset, greeting their neighbors. Many dressed up for church on Sundays, rested afterwards. We attended a small service, trying to catch the jist of the message in Spanish.

One night we strolled the beach and sat near a hippy group who were chatting, strumming a guitar. Some had been taking drugs and drinking. One girl began pleading for help, for someone to lead her to a bathroom. A friend helped her…we walked on in the dark, sobered. "Why would people try to enlarge pleasure with drugs?" I wondered to Zachary. "God has so much joy for us. He is Joy."

"That's right. They just don't know Him yet."

"I want to know better how to tell them."

Leaving Spain, we followed the Riviera coastline past Marseille to Monaco and on to Italy. I had read about the Renaissance artistry of Florence…now I wanted to see it. And we were not disappointed. Walking though the city thronged with tourists, we stood in line to see Michelangelo's marble statue of David. When we arrived I was entranced. Was David going to step off his pedestal? He seemed almost alive.

The Ponte Vecchio Bridge over the Arno River was a focal point of the city. We rested on the bridge at the foot of Benvenuto Cellini's statue one hot afternoon, and I breathed a deep sigh of contentment. "It's so fulfilling to be here, Zach. This place was an epicenter of Europe in the Renaissance. But Savonarola their famous preacher they burned at the stake in the square near here. Incredible."

"Yes, it's amazing," he agreed. "Such history, architecture, bronze statues…"

Cycling southward to Rome we drove by the hilltop town of Narni, and decided to stay there for the night. Narni, like Narnia, I decided, was an enchanted place. The old post office at the top of the hill happened to also house a small hotel. So we checked in, found a restaurant to eat in, and later climbed between thick sheets of linen in our little room, grateful and exhausted. The next morning I looked out the window down, down to a deep ravine. "Look!" I exclaimed. "We're perched on a cliff, and there's a train winding down the valley." I watched the train chug through the blue shadows. Later over a sunny breakfast I told Zach, "Someday we have to come back here."

After driving through the vast city of Rome we chose to head south to Lido di Ostia and camp on the beach. For several days we took the train to the city, and visited the Vatican and its treasures, the Sistine Chapel, Spanish Steps, Pantheon, the Roman Forum of ruins....the Coliseum.

Packing up, we rode north to Venice, to Austria, west to Germany, then down through Switzerland, the Alps blazing with glory. And across France again, the Channel, and up into London.

We arrived saddle sore in London one night, determined not to spend much money on a hotel. It was late... we finally climbed the iron fence into Hyde Park, and spread our sleeping bags under a large tree. We prayed for protection, and the next morning a police bobby genially unlocked an iron gate so we could exit the park.

Through the trip we had occasionally camped, stayed a few nights in youth hostels, but mostly we tried to find cheap bed and breakfasts. After a munching on coffee and rolls at a hotel we would usually buy bread, cheese, fruit, and coke for lunch on the road, then feast at a reasonable restaurant at night. We did manage to only spend about $5 a day, following our faithful guidebook.

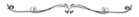

With inquiry we found shipping for the 650cc Bonneville to New York City, paying to have them crate it up. We then had several days before our flight to New York City. Wandering London's streets I observed the centuries compressed into space with blocks of ordered, blackened buildings, and the decadence of culture. Indeed, across all of Europe we saw cathedrals and churches admired, but mostly devoid of worshippers.

"Why has Europe kept its quaintness and beauty, but lost its awe of God," I wondered to Zach. "This imprint of God's glory is everywhere, but the heart of God's purpose, the breath of the Holy Spirit seems to have almost left."

"Maybe they stopped praying or reading their Bibles much, and just got cold," he suggested.

"God, infuse them with fresh Life!"

SUNLIGHT DANCING ON THE CEILING

We flew back to New York City, picked up our motorcycle from the docks and rode it to Buffalo, where Uncle Dewey and Aunt Petey welcomed us with a great meal, cozy bedroom, and an openness to hear our tales of travel. Next we drove on to Mom and Dad's university apartment in Ann Arbor, Michigan, where Dad was enjoying his PhD program. Dan and David were 14 and 12 years old now. They listened to our adventures, then told their own.

"We were worried about you after you crossed the Channel into France," Mom exclaimed. "Several postcards came from England and then nothing for weeks! We were praying a lot. Finally we started getting postcards again. I guess the mail from the Continent is slower."

Cycling on to Minnesota, we arrived as fall semester was beginning-- and St. Paul Bible College had moved! It was now west of the Twin Cities, on a former Jesuit campus near St. Bonifacius. And the college's name was to be changed to Crown College! We found a one bedroom upstairs apartment next to a small lake in Excelsior. There were large trees and rippling waves right outside our windows. In the mornings I would wake to dancing sunlight on the ceiling--the waves reflecting golden rays. Throughout the year (when there were no clouds, and no frozen ice) my spirit lifted with the lilting sunshine.

We sold the trusty Bonneville cycle to pay for tuition, then both looked for work to pay living expenses--Zach in construction, me in nursing. We only had Zach's white truck for transportation, so my work needed to be close to the apartment. And incredibly, I found part time employment at a doctor's office right across the street.

It was wonderful to be a student, with no dorm rules. I especially enjoyed the missions class taught by Dr. Conley our mentor-friend. I had confidence, purpose, even delight in life. For awhile I got up very early to meet with the Lord, even though I was a night owl.

Zach's carpentry work was erratic, so we prayed for regular work for him. And I tried to show God's love at the clinic, to be consistent.

The year passed quickly. One afternoon in second semester we interviewed with Dr. LeRoy Johnston as missionary candidates with the Christian and Missionary Alliance. I was curious about the process and expectations. Dr. Johnston was young and thick bearded--even though it was against our Bible college rules to have a beard--and he was warm, interested in us. But it was clear from the interview that he cared about Zach's credentials and application more than mine. I was the wife who would follow along and support Zachary's ministry.

Each senior was given opportunity to give their personal testimony during one morning chapel…and I was gratified to share my journey. The Lord had been so faithful to lead me from spiritual babyhood in Homejo to this point where I could launch with my husband into ministry.

My family, Zach's family were all there when we walked down the chapel aisle to receive our diplomas at graduation. Grandma and Grandpa Hofer hosted a sumptuous reception for us all soon afterwards…and Zach and I prayed over our next step. The Alliance required two years of home service before we could be sent to the mission field. Where in the States could we serve?

One evening I mentioned to Zach, "I noticed a small card posted on the campus bulletin board to recruit workers for Child Evangelism Crusade in Kingman, Arizona. Your parents would love to have us near them in Arizona for awhile. Maybe we should call the number and check it out."

"Sure, why don't you call them."

The lady who answered sounded older. "Yes, I would love to have a young couple working with me. Let me know when you can come and visit."

Again, we decided to motorcycle…it was so much cheaper, and more fun! Browsing, looking at different styles and makes we settled on a 950cc Harley Sportster…loaded it with a banana seat, a chopped front end, and a tail light in the shape of a Jerusalem cross. It was hot! And it came with with a monthly payment.

The trip down to Arizona was both exhilarating and tiring. We had engine trouble south of Denver and spread sleeping bags in a piney rest area near Larkspur. The next morning we rumbled into Colorado Springs where a friendly young mechanic named Jim let Zach borrow tools to work on the cycle himself. The work took hours, and Jim went beyond the call of duty. "You guys can stay with my wife and me. We rent nearby, and have a spare bedroom."

"Wow," Zach replied. "Thanks so much!"

We walked to their white painted home where four dogs shared the fenced front yard. Jim and Julie looked like a hippy Romeo and Juliet. Julie was six months pregnant--pretty, with long dark hair--managing well with limited resources.

"We want to find 10 acres out east on the plains, where we can have room for our dogs to run," Jim confided over supper.

"That's great," I said. "The view of the mountains is beautiful. Our dream is to help out with a ministry here in the States for two years, and then live overseas. I grew up among tribespeople in New Guinea, so we'll probably end up there."

"Yeah. Marti's a nurse, and I'm a builder, so we can give practical help," Zach added. "And we'd also teach people about Jesus."

"Are you guys Christians?" I asked. "Do you know the Lord in your hearts?"

"Not really," Jim answered. "We're not church goers, but we like to help people."

"Well, you've sure helped us," Zach declared. "We're really grateful. But you should read the Bible sometimes, check out a good church."

"We'll pray you find one...and that you get your 10 acres on the plains!"

"Thank you," Julie said, smiling at me.

The next day, while Zach and Jim were at the cycle shop I wandered in downtown Colorado Springs, walking around the large square and in front of the courthouse. In 1971 it was a nice sized city—not too big, solid, friendly, rather frontier-like, with Pikes Peak rising west to a height of 14,000 feet. I little dreamed that someday this area would be my long term home.

After two nights the Sportster was fixed, and thanking Jim and Julie profusely, we headed for Phoenix, to Mom and Dad home in Scottsdale. Their home on the winding canal, had a view of the distant blue-purple mountains.

"Welcome!" Dad greeted us. They were excited that we would check out the ministry in Kingman, 40 miles north. It would be so good to live near family, since my parents were heading back to Irian Jaya.

Our few days in Kingman proved interesting as we got to know Miss Harvey in charge of Child Evangelism. She had two large mobile homes parked near each other. One was stocked full of supplies, the other she lived in. That weekend she wanted to reach out to children at the county fair.

"Would you two be willing to dress up like clowns and bring the children in?" she queried. "I have the costumes and face paint."

"Sure," Zach laughed. I was more hesitant. I had never been a clown before!

It was quite an experience. Bright garbed, and with our faces painted we wandered through the fairgrounds inviting children to our tent where Miss Harvey would share Bible stories, then invite each child to accept Jesus into their heart. About 10 to 20 children came through, and some accepted the Lord.

We rode back to Phoenix a little dubious about the adventure. Who would disciple those children? Wouldn't it be better to reach the parents with Bible truth first? Mom and Dad Noll appreciated our reasoning, and after prayer Zach and I decided to head back to Minnesota and interview for church openings with the district superintendent in St. Paul.

The choices of our lives lead us in unexpected ways. I had no idea that the next open door I passed through would change the whole course of my life.

Rev. Leo Bereth in St. Paul did have a church opening for us. "It's on the edge of White Earth Indian Reservation up north, west of Bemidji," he said. "Rather like a missions outreach, really. An older man has renovated the church in the hamlet of Ebro, and a Bible school student is filling in on Sundays…there are just a handful of people attending. There is a parsonage near to it that you could renovate and live in. Are you interested in checking it out?"

"Sure!" Zach replied. "It sounds like a good opportunity."

So one fall weekend Zach and I, Mom and Dad, and Grandpa Hofer drove north to Ebro.

I was excited as we drove by forest and fields from Bagley to Ebro. What would this hamlet be like? The sorrel bushes by the side of the road had turned red. Gold and green meadows rolled out on either side of this road as we turned south, and then we passed scattered trees...and there was Ebro! A few houses, a tiny post office, a curve in the road, and a railroad track we bumped over.

"Was that it?" I asked, surprised.

"It must be. We have to cross back and turn south before the railroad tracks," Zach said. We turned around and drove slowly up a graveled road, past a few houses. There on the right was a neat brown church, and farther up the hill a parsonage with peeling white paint, set against green pines.

We parked in the grassy field near the church and walked in. The whitewashed sanctuary had rich brown beams crisscrossing the raised ceiling, and two rows of wooden pews. There were five women and children in the pews, with a young preacher at the pulpit. He greeted us and continued the service.

I breathed deeply. Was this our new home? An outpost among whites and Ojibwe (Chippewa) native Americans, next to railroad tracks? I did like frontiers. And tribes people. It would be adventurous. Maybe I could find a small hospital to work in.

We drove back to the Twin Cities, prayed more, and accepted the assignment. Zach and I committed to two years of pastoring the church at Ebro, building up God's little flock.

When we packed up our belongings at the Excelsior apartment, the sunlight shimmered on the ceiling. It danced and cavorted, bounced, and laughed, reflecting the dancing waves. "I'm going to miss this special home!" I told Zachary. "I loved our last year of Bible college, and living near my family after they moved here from Michigan.

"Yeah, it's been special. But we'll have an adventure up north. It'll be good too."

A PASTOR'S WIFE

This new stage of life was a dramatic shift. For years I had been receiving instruction and discipleship. Now for two years Zach and I were responsible to take leadership of this church in northern Minnesota. We were to care for others rather than receive care. I was ready mentally, but sometimes emotionally I felt at loose ends.

We found a blue and white mobile home to rent in a trailer park on the west end of Bagley. It was about 8 feet wide, 50 feet long, with a compact turquoise kitchen, a bath, and two tiny bedrooms. I made it homey with our small blue couch and a few pictures...and even taped a poster of Butch Cassidy and the Sundance Kid (with Etta) to the refrigerator for dramatic effect! In another place I taped a poster of a girl walking down railroad tracks into the distance. I was here, but someday we would be moving on.

We began to visit the homes in Ebro and make friends with the native American and white settlers. Some homes were neat and clean, others dirty, with junk piled in their yards. Grandma Watnous was one of the oldest residents, a Norwegian who had prayed and supported the church for years. She lived with her daughter and son-in-law now (who didn't go to church), and shared her heart with us over coffee. "I prayed for a young couple to come," she confided, "because I want more youth to come to the church."

"Well, thank you, Grandma," I answered. "We're here because you prayed!"

We had examined the parsonage on the rise behind the church. It had been empty for awhile, and had no indoor bathroom. Zach was to gut most of the house and build a bathroom and laundry addition on the south side. The Alliance mission fund would supply materials. So for months Zachary was busy at the parsonage, driving back and forth in our white truck.

When Mom and Dad headed back with Dan and Dave to Irian Jaya we drove to the Twin Cities to see them off. There were so many goodbyes on the earth! I hugged them with tears. But I was happily married now, and trusting to possibly arrive in Irian Jaya as a mission worker myself.

They gave us their sleek car to drive, so now with wheels I could find a nursing job.

The small hospital in Bagley had no openings, but Fosston, west of Ebro (and 18 miles from Bagley) had a part time evening charge nurse position. I was elated but nervous—I would be the only RN on that shift at the 35 bed hospital, with an LPN to distribute meds, and three nursing assistants. Was I responsible enough to be in charge of the emergency room and the only RN to help deliver babies with the doctor? What if a patient died on my shift!

The older nurses oriented me well, and I took charge with trepidation. When we did have a mother in labor the nursing assistants who had worked there for years were helpful. "I think it's time to call the doctor," one murmured to me. "She's had several babies, and she's moving fast."

There were three doctors who admitted patients—all brothers, older men who had grown up in the community and followed in their physician father's footsteps. All three were considerate, and the oldest Dr. George Sather took a kindly interest in me.

As weeks passed Zachary and I made friends in the community. Some were neighbors like the Lambs who lived across from the church. Leo was white, Mary Jane Ojibwe Indian, and their eight children rambunctious and loveable. They began to come to church as did Buck and Bonnie and their four kids. Bonnie was Ojibwe, newly come back to the Lord. She had been raised by two missionary women, and was determined to follow God now, as was Buck.

Josh and Leota Dahl and their seven children began showing up at the little church on Sundays and were such an encouragement to us. Josh owned the plumbing shop in Bagley and helped with the parsonage addition. He was not a Christian yet, by his own admission. Leota was hungry for more of the Holy Spirit, so we began having Bible studies at their large home outside of Bagley.

God brought friendships, practical help, and the anointing of His Spirit. In the Sunday services Zach led worship on the guitar, preached sincerely, and I taught Sunday school in the side room. Each Sunday I registered the number of people who came in a little brown book, and rejoiced to see the increase.

Meanwhile autumn's red and gold leaves fell, the meadows were frosty in the mornings, and nights became bitter cold. Sometimes clouds were gray and lowering for days, and my outlook would grow dim, limited, despite the growth in the church. It was like walking through a wilderness, a low depressed area where all around the horizon looked the same.

"What are we accomplishing in this community?" I wondered one day to Zach. "Progress is slow...even if all the people came on a single Sunday, we wouldn't fill the church. And I miss classes, the activity of college life. Many people here haven't been educated beyond high school—some haven't even graduated from that! I feel isolated...I miss our old friends!"

"Yeah, I miss our friends too, especially the motorcycle guys. But we are making new ones. And we're learning how to disciple people. Buck and Bonnie have made progress, and look how the home group at Josh and Leota's is growing. We're sowing seeds. And some people are watching, even if we don't know it. We need to be patient."

"Shall we take Mondays off instead of Saturdays and drive east to Bemidji? You always have to study for the sermon on Saturday anyway. On Mondays we could browse at the library, go out to eat, have a change of scenery in a bigger town."

"Sure, that's a good idea. Maybe you wouldn't feel so isolated then."

And Zach prayed with me, "Lord, help Marti to be happy in your work. Give us love for all the people, help us to be content."

"Yes, God," I agreed. "Each person in this community is precious. Help us to see each one as you do, and know how to serve them."

But Dan didn't always want to pray together. At one point of discouragement I looked over the horizon spiritually and considered leaving God's will. "I always wanted to be a flight attendant," I thought. "What if I left and did just that! I could travel all over the world, life would be so much more exciting."

After thinking about it carefully I realized that leaving God's will for me would mean saying no to Him and walking into darkness. Inwardly, I could see it....walking stubbornly from light into a cloud of darkness. I had a will...I could choose to leave, to make my own way.

And I knew it was dangerous. If I left God, I had no guarantee I could come back whenever I wanted. The Holy Spirit has to draw a person, I knew. In the end I chose to hang on in obedience, and I had peace.

NEW LIFE

Into the gray winter wilderness life slowly began to spring forth. First, I found out I was pregnant. In a few weeks severe nausea set in and I stayed in bed a lot, lost weight. But the church continued to grow. Leota and her daughters capably took over the Sunday school, and visiting ministers encouraged us. Ray and Petra Arno from Alaska drove in and preached, and Rev. Bereth the district superintendent, with his wife.

"We pastored in this area years ago when we were starting out," he told us. "It brings back a lot of memories!"

Christmas and a Nativity program, New Years... and more families came. We kept meeting for prayer at Leota's house, asking God for a move of His Spirit. Leota got filled with the Holy Spirit and spoke in tongues! And we prayed for the gifts of the Holy Spirit to operate in Ebro Community Church. And the Lord did move...some Sundays the worship was so long and fervent that Zach preached short, or not at all. The Holy Spirit spoke in the service through tongues and interpretation, and in prophecy. I was amazed and encouraged--I was even used in prophecy!

The baby grew within me, I began to feel movement. "Lord, use this little one for your glory," I prayed, laying hands on my swelling body. I bought maternity clothes and loose nursing uniforms, wore my long hair down with a blue bandana above my bangs, and tiny hoop earrings. I began to waddle slightly, as the pregnancy lengthened. Bonnie and I sometimes met in Ebro to walk the railroad tracks for exercise, and prayed.

Zach kept working on the parsonage...taping, painting, installing kitchen cupboards, and a large window nook with table and benches. "We'll someday sit there over morning coffee and watch snow fall in the woods beyond," I said. "And our baby will be sleeping in another room. It'll have blue eyes, like you."

"Yes," Zachary replied, hugging me. "We'll be a family, in this house. What names do you like?"

"Well, we talked about Nicholas, after your grandfather."

"Nicholas has a good ring to it. What about a girl? I like the name Susanne."

I considered. "That sounds old to me. How about Tania? Tania Noelle!"

'Hmmm.' Maybe. "I'd better get back to work. I'd like us to be here in this parsonage before the baby comes."

The living and dining room Zach had opened into one great room. He lined one long wall with rich stained boards against which I hung lacey white curtains. We bought a small wood stove to sit in front of, and painted the adjoining bedroom light green. (The upstairs would be finished later.) The entry/laundry and the bathroom were nearly completed. We were going to be new parents and live in a newly finished parsonage!

We heard about a large conference Campus Crusade was sponsoring in Dallas: Explo '72. Young people were gathering from all over the country, and each night there would be a huge meeting in the Cotton Bowl. I was excited.

"Zach, do you think we could go to Explo '72? I'd be seven months pregnant, so we couldn't ride the cycle. We'd have to take the car. Let's pray about it."

"Well, that'd be special. It'd be good to get more spiritual input. I could ask someone to preach for me the Sunday we're gone."

We had peace to go, and enough money for registration, gas, and food. I was occasionally uncomfortable during the long drive, but the big issue was where we could stay—we had limited funds for motels. After standing in long lines to register, we made friends with Dave and Tony, two hippy motorcycle guys, and all of us were given housing in an elegant suburban home for several nights. "How blessed we are," I thought, as I fell asleep on our comfortable bed beneath a thick coverlet. And with white carpet, too!

When our nights at the luxury home were completed another family welcomed us in…and through all the days we heard good teachings with amazing nights of worship and preaching at the Cotton Bowl—including hearing Bill Bright, the leader of Campus Crusade.

"I like the preaching," I told Zach, "but what impresses me most is the freedom in worship each evening. I've never been in a gathering where thousands of young people worshipped wholeheartedly, so many with their hands raised. You feel God so much!"

Zach nodded. "It is terrific. I had no idea it would be this great."

As we hung out with Dave and Tony from California, they began to feel burdened for our church. "Why don't you come back with us, visit the service, and pray for us!" Dan suggested.

The guys thought about it." That's a good idea," Dave said.

"You could ride with us, but we'd need to rent a trailer for your cycles."

"We'll see how much it costs to rent one," Tony said.

On the last night after the closing song I was a little sad to leave the huge gathering. We descended the tiers of seats, and as I turned to go out one of the exits, the Lord spoke to me. "Turn around and look," He said.

I turned around. Many of the tiers were empty, but a cluster of young people up and across from me caught my eye. I watched for awhile. One young man with longish blond hair laughed, raised his hands over his head, and brought them down for emphasis. He stood out to me. I turned back, not comprehending any significance, and thought, "I must have heard wrong."

Years later the Lord reminded me of this incident, and I made the connection. Pastor Ted Haggard of New Life Church in Colorado Springs had gotten saved at Explo '72. The Lord knew I would someday be a part of that church…and He showed me Ted that night, a teenager.

Our ride home to Minnesota was filled with joking and songs. Especially from Dave, who had sandy, long hair. Tony was dark, shorter, more thoughtful and quiet. Dave would break out singing, then remonstrate us. "You guys need to loosen up and sing out more!"

I agreed with him. Driving north through miles of field and forest, we began to worship loudly, and be filled with joy.

BIRTHING LAUGHTER

Dave and Tony stayed a few weeks, and during those days they hung out with young people, invited them to church, did spiritual warfare…and the church began to get crowded! Experienced musicians joined Zach on the praise team, so the quality and intensity of our worship increased.

I was due to deliver toward the end of July…Zach was working hard to finish the parsonage. After Dave and Tony left, Zach called Grandpa Hofer. "Can you come up and help me for a week or two, Grandpa? I have several projects to finish on the parsonage."

"Sure, Zachary. I'll drive up next Monday."

Grandpa was with us about a week. The evening of July 21 he went to bed early after a hard day's work, and Zach and I served coffee to a few Lamb family teenagers who had dropped in to chat. I began to cramp and feel uncomfortable. After they left Zach drove me to Fosston Hospital around midnight.

Dr. George Sather was on call, and I was grateful. The nurses were my friends, so we chatted as they admitted me. When stage three set in and I was pushing, they were all business. Around 5am Nicholas Lee was born…7 lbs., 2 oz., with loud, healthy squalls.

"Call the dad in," Dr. George ordered.

"You have a healthy boy, Zachary!"

Zach's blue eyes sparkled. He stood on one foot and laughed for pure joy as they held Nick up ruddy, with wisps of blond hair. "What a great little man!"

But I was on the delivery table for awhile. I kept bleeding, the nurses kept massaging my abdomen, taking my blood pressure. Dr. George kept his hand on my arm, asking every few minutes, "How do you feel?" Finally I stabilized, and after receiving three pints of blood felt alert again.

When we held Nick later in my hospital room it was with wonder. How could a miniature human be formed so perfectly, with everything working!

Grandpa Hofer saw his great-grandson, and then drove home to St. Paul. We called Zach's parents, then telegrammed my parents, with a reference to Psalm 128 (NIV) which ends with:

"May the Lord bless you from Zion all the days of your life; may you see the prosperity of Jerusalem, and may you live to see your children's children. Peace be upon Israel!"

In a few days Zach brought me home. He had been working on the parsonage, and hadn't set up the crib. "Why isn't Nick's crib ready?" I exclaimed, exasperated.

"I just didn't get to it. The Lamb boys borrowed the truck and will bring it back tomorrow—I left the crib hardware in it by mistake.

"I can't believe you forgot. A crib is kind of important."

"Well, I'm sorry. I've been working on the parsonage, running back and forth."

So the first night we slept with Nick between us. He woke every two hours, needing to nurse….we were both exhausted.

Our second and third nights were better. Zach set the crib up in the tiny second bedroom, and we began to try to form a schedule. This little bundle of joy took huge amounts of time and energy.

Zach finished the parsonage about three weeks later, and Leota and her daughters helped us move. I was grateful, still a little weak, but our first night in the new parsonage was special. "We're here, we're really in our new home!" I exclaimed. Nick's crib was in a corner of our bedroom, with all of the furniture in place on the main floor.

Unpacking a few boxes we sat at the kitchen nook to eat a light supper. We could look west toward the dark forest where the sun was setting behind the pines. Long sunbeams slanted into our gold kitchen, glinting off the glasses of milk, and Zach's gold wedding band. Nick was sleeping peacefully. Zach prayed over the meal. "Thank you, Lord for bringing us here, for taking care of us. Thank you for Nicky, for our new home…and for this food. Help us to fulfill your will here."

"Amen," I agreed.

STORM WARNINGS

Almost a year of pastoring was behind us, and now we had a new baby. I looked forward to one more year of nurturing the church and our son…and then on to mission work somewhere overseas. Irian Jaya, I hoped.

I tried to order my world with routine and order, expecting good results. At three months Nick was on a schedule, everything was unpacked. Mary Lamb, the pretty twelve year old Ojibwe girl down the hill came to babysit for me occasionally, and she was lavish with admiration. "This house is very pretty! You have a nice husband and new baby, and the church is growing…you must be so happy!"

"Thank you, Mary. Yes, I should be happy and so grateful, but somehow I feel unsettled. I don't know why."

I felt secure in home and calling, but in another way I could not rest. Perhaps it was because Zachary seemed restless, unfocused, though he loved holding Nick.

What was wrong? Zach kept pastoring the church, but not with the same zeal as before. He seemed distant, aloof, preoccupied. He didn't seem as interested in reading the Bible, certainly didn't want to pray together. I noticed he began tuning in to secular music on the radio, rather than Christian. He wanted to take walks in the woods alone to think, but wouldn't want to talk about it later.

The more introspective he became, the more persistent and questioning I was. But he wouldn't open up to me. I began to put Nick in the baby backpack and take walks to Bonnie's home down the hill, past Myra's house. Myra was an attractive Ojibwe woman in her early 20's who had never been married. She had three cute daughters, and Bonnie had recently led her to the Lord.

Buck and Bonnie were faithfully coming to church and inviting others. Her older kids would watch Nick while Bonnie and I walked the railroad tracks and prayed. We prayed for the church, for Bonnie's four other children that her ex-husband was raising, for finances, work for Buck, and for our marriages. This prayer with Bonnie and also with Leota (when I saw her in town), meant a lot to me.

Eventually I went back to my part time evening nursing at Fosston Hospital. Zach was going to watch Nick the three evenings a week I was gone, but when Nick was fussy, Zach got frustrated.

"Sometimes I don't know how to keep him from crying," he explained. "And in the afternoons I have other work to do."

"Well, I've heard that Myra would be willing to babysit some," I replied. "Maybe you could pick him up after work around dinnertime, from her house."

And so it was arranged. Only sometimes Zachary got home not long before I did at midnight. He would visit with Myra and her brother most of the evening, with Nick there.

The church continued to slowly grow. Zach began working on the upstairs of the parsonage during the day, and some evenings we would have the Bible study in our new home.

One night over supper he mentioned, "This church in the Twin Cities wants to send a college work group up over Thanksgiving. They could help gut the upstairs, and it would speed up the renovation process. We could use the extra help."

"Where would they stay?" I questioned.

"They could stay here, bring their sleeping bags. I can help with the Thanksgiving dinner."

"I don't know, Zachary. I'm barely managing with Nick, the church, and my work at the hospital...a crew like that to host seems overwhelming!"

As Thanksgiving approached I grew more nervous about the young people coming. "I just can't do it, Zach. I feel overwhelmed. Maybe I should take Nick and visit Romaine in St. Paul over this holiday. You could host the group yourself."

"Alright...I don't mind."

Bonnie offered to ride with me the 250 miles to the Twin Cities. She had pastor friends on the way, in Elk River, and we could stay with them one night. The evening we stayed with them I shared my concerns about Zach and me with the pastor and his wife, and the four of us prayed.

Later the next day I found Romaine's house in St. Paul--she rented the second floor of a steep roofed home, and had decorated it charmingly. We had fun together, enjoying Nick, sharing stories, and had a potluck Thanksgiving with a few of her friends.

When it came time to drive home I was refreshed.

CHRISTMAS IN THE PARSONAGE

Our weekly routine resumed with Sunday services, Zachary's remodeling of the upstairs parsonage, my evening hospital shifts, and our caring for Nick. He was chubby and cuddly, and when I slipped him into yellow terrycloth pajamas he looked like an adorable duckling with downy hair! I continued to nurse him, and supplement with cereal at night so he would sleep longer.

Zach and I delighted in Nick, and we enjoyed romantic times together, but our closeness ended there. I longed to intercede together, but Zach generally refused. He would rather just pray over meals.

Christmas was coming, and Mom and Dad Smith arrived to celebrate. We decorated a long needled pine tree and strung it with lights, the red Christmas balls from our wedding, and silver icicles. Nick loved the tree and kept pushing up to it in his walker, reaching for balls and flinching when the sharp needles pricked him.

When Mom and Dad arrived Nick was the center of attention. Their first grandchild... and his first Christmas! Dad delighted in walking Nick to sleep, and Mom hovered like a mother hen. "Watch out, Bob! His little arm is stretched over your shoulder, and it might be hurting." Dad gently pulled Nick's arm back, and kept walking.

Since the upstairs was unfinished the Mom and Dad opted to stay at a hotel in town, but they enjoyed meals with us, the church program, Zach's preaching, and were curious about the baptism in the Holy Spirit. Zachary had not experienced this himself, and we all discussed Baptist vs. Charismatic theology.

When they left we were laden with gifts, including an expensive camera I could learn to use. One day Myra came up to the parsonage…she asked if I would take pictures of her. We took several, and I later gave her copies.

I continued to work the 3-11:30 shift several days a week, and Myra kept babysitting Nick in the early evenings. Becoming more proficient as a nurse, I worked at the front desk with a heart monitor nearby--all of the RN's were freshly trained in cardiac monitoring in the early 1970's. One night my patient went into ventricular fibrillation so the LPN and I used the defibrillator to zap his heart, and did CPR until Dr. Sather arrived.

Most evenings were quiet, and I could spend some time with each patient. One older man was on IVs, slowly dying. He loved the Lord, and his face radiated deep joy when talking about Heaven. "Max, if you see Jesus before I do, give Him a big hug for me!" I told him.

"I will," he replied. Heaven seemed closer with Max around.

In northern Minnesota the temperature would dip far below zero, so in the hospital parking lot there were plugs to use for our car engine heaters. We all wanted our cars to start at 11:40 at night when we drove home! This one icy night I dressed warm, heated the car after my shift, and headed the fifteen miles east to Ebro. A few miles out of town I hit a patch of ice on a downward slope… foolishly braked…and the car fishtailed, then hurtled end over end in the median, landing upside down on a bank of soft snow.

Crying out "God--help me!" my life actually passed before my eyes. I landed pinned between the headrest and roof of the car, since I wasn't wearing a seatbelt. The car was upside down, wheels in the air, with the engine running. I was alive! I twisted loose to turn off the engine, then reached out of the smashed window.

A passing trucker stopped and helped pull me out of the car. I was shaky, jangled. But I was whole, with only a scratch on my arm! "Thank you, Lord," I cried hoarsely. The man offered to take me in his truck, so I reached for my purse, and he drove me back to Fosston Hospital. Dr. George was there as I walked in. He was comforting, and I telephoned Zach to pick me up.

I was dazed on the ride home in Zachary's truck. When we went to bed he held me close. "You could have been killed!" he said. "I'm so thankful you weren't hurt." His attention reassured me, gave me hope of spiritual intimacy and communion.

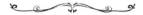

In a few weeks the gold Maverick was fixed—Buck, Bonnie's husband, did auto body work, so we paid him to repair the damage with insurance money. I was so grateful…but our marriage was no better. Outwardly life went on normally, but inwardly something was broken. Zach didn't share his heart with me, and when I got insistent he either got angry or withdrew.

Slowly I became demanding, controlling…he retreated more, walked around depressed. What could I do? I suggested we drive to St Paul to get help from Rev. Hall who had counseled us, performed the wedding ceremony. Zachary refused.

One day after a huge argument, Zach put on a thick army overcoat and announced he was leaving. "Where are you going?" I asked.

"I don't know. I'm just going off for awhile. I'll hitchhike. I want to be alone."

I watched anxiously as he bundled up with hat and gloves. "Goodbye," he said gruffly. "I'll see you in a few days."

That night I prayed long and desperately, and the next day zipped Nick up in his blue bunting and drove to Bagley to see Leota. She put her arm around me and we prayed fervently. I had peace, but I felt like I was walking a tightrope high above my circumstances. If I kept my eyes on the Lord I was alright. If I looked down, wondering where Zach was, and what would happen, I got sick with worry.

Another day I visited Bonnie down the hill, and we prayed. "Marti," she confided, "I think I should warn you about Myra. There's something going on between her and Zach. You should watch out."

I was shocked. "Bonnie, do you really think he'd be interested in her? I know she's pretty and likes to have fun. But she hasn't graduated from high school, she's on welfare, she's never been married and has three kids!"

"You should be aware—pray about it!"

I nodded, a little baffled. If there was another woman, I didn't think it would be Myra. Bonnie helped lift Nick into the baby carrier on my back, and I trudged back to the parsonage. The afternoon was cold and gray. Wind rushed through the pines behind our house, and waved the meadow grasses at my feet. I was lonely. I wished my parents were closer.

"God, take care of Zachary. Bring him home...I bind the darkness away from him in Jesus' name."

I fixed supper for me, and fed Nick his baby food. He grinned crookedly and crowed. Wiping his face, I lifted him out of the high chair and hugged him. After changing him into pajamas I rocked him as he sucked his bottle, and sang him a lullaby. Then I tucked him into his crib in the corner of our bedroom. Later, sitting up in bed I read the Bible.

"The Lord is nigh unto those who are of a broken heart, and saveth such as be of a contrite spirit. Many are the afflictions of the righteous; but the Lord delivereth him out of them all." Ps. 34:18, 19 (KJV)

After reading a few chapters I shared my heart with the Lord, listened for His voice. He was with me in the room. I snapped off the light, turned over, and went to sleep.

Zach arrived in the front yard in a few days, his face chapped with cold. My relief was profound. A chasm of horror was closed—he was home!

He didn't have much to say, but seemed more at peace. "I shared my heart with a few people I hitchhiked with," he told me. "I decided to come home."

In a few weeks Zach said he wanted to resign from the church. "I don't feel I'm equipped to lead these people. I'm struggling spiritually myself. I don't know what to do. I've been a builder...maybe I should go back to school and get a degree in engineering."

Alarmed and perplexed, I hesitated before answering. "Well, we need to work on our marriage. Maybe we should move down to the Twin Cities and make plans from there. You know I want to do mission work like we planned, but we could delay things for awhile."

The next Sunday Zachary resigned from Ebro Community Church. He was going to write a letter to Rev. Bereth. But there was no one to take his place on Sundays, so he kept leading, kept preaching. Finally we made plans to visit Zach's parents in Arizona. They would watch Nick for a few days, and we could travel to California and motorcycle up the coast. Maybe a fun vacation would help heal our marriage.

ENTERING THE WHIRLWIND

I awoke early the day before we were to leave. Pulling on a warm robe I slid into the kitchen nook and opened my Bible. The polished wood reflected the faint morning light. Flicking on a small lamp I opened to Isaiah where I had been reading a lot from lately. Chapter 57 rebuked false leaders, and ended with:

> *"I have seen his ways, and will heal him; I will lead him also, and restore comforts unto him and to his mourners. I create the fruit of the lips. Peace, peace to him that is far off, and to him that is near, saith the Lord, and I will heal him. But the wicked are like the troubled sea, when it cannot rest, whose waters cast up mire and dirt. There is no peace, saith my God, to the wicked." Is. 57:18-21 (KJV)*

Somehow the words seemed prophetic.

Zach walked into the kitchen. "I've been thinking…it's not too cold today. I'll ride the motorcycle to Bemidji and have it checked out before we load it up to haul to Arizona. We want to have it running good for our trip to California."

"That's a good idea, Honey. I'm going to wash clothes and pack for our trip. "Drive carefully! I'm going back to bed till Nicky wakes up."

Later in the morning Zach roared off, warmly dressed. I cleaned the house, washed clothes, packed our suitcases. Nick pushed around in his stroller in bib overalls. Every day he was cuter as his short blond hair grew. His strong chortle and wide smile engaged whoever he met.

Evening shadows lengthened and Zach did not arrive. I began to worry. Why didn't he telephone?

After supper I put Nick to bed, ironed, and began my last load of clothes. Somehow the washer hookup broke loose and flooded the

Marti Anderson

laundry room. Disgruntled, I began mopping up, praying. "Lord, please protect Zachary. Wherever he is, keep him safe...bring him home!" I began weeping, kept praying. I called a couple of friends, and then went to bed around midnight.

Waking early I decided to call Leota. Maybe Zach had been in an accident! She agreed to drive to Bemidji with me to search for him. I dropped Nick off with her daughters and we drove east through pines and sunlit meadows, watching for any broken down cycle by the side of the road. We drove around town and ended up at Myra's parents' house. Her mom answered the door. "He was here, but he went home this morning," she said.

"Thank you," I said shakily. "Thanks so much."

Leota and I drove home soberly. "Why didn't he call," I wondered out loud. We prayed, I dropped her off at her house, and picked up Nick.

Reaching Ebro, I saw that the churchyard had cars parked in it. This was Sunday afternoon, April 1....were they having a special meeting? I walked into the church, and people greeted me awkwardly. They had been having a meeting to discuss Zach and future leadership. They looked at me sympathetically.

Zachary drove up to the parsonage sometime after I reached home. He walked into the entryway, the clean laundry room where I had mopped up water the night before. He was quiet, tentative.

"Where were you last night?"

"The cycle had some problems. I stayed at Myra's parents' house."

I hitched myself up onto the washer, looked him in the eye. "Was Myra there? Did you sleep with her?"

"Yeah."

I doubled over, the words sinking in. If he had plunged a knife into my abdomen I couldn't have been more horrified.

"You slept with her!" I jumped off the washer in anguish. "How could you?"

He hesitated. "I know it was wrong. I shouldn't have. I took her for a ride before we left and then there was cycle trouble. And I stayed the night."

102

I didn't know what to do. He seemed relieved to have told the truth, and I was in agony. Numb with shock and horror. And wounded, torn inwardly so that I felt like I could slowly bleed to death if left alone. What could I do?

Later we left Nick with neighbors and took a drive, a walk in the woods. Wandering wordlessly through trees and brush, we stopped suddenly. A little mouse scampered, cute and furry, wary of us. We had always liked watching small wild animals. This interruption was an island of normalcy in the midst of a whirlwind of pain. The attention drew us together…we stood close, touching.

And then the animal ran away, and the pain returned.

In a couple of days there was a church meeting where Zach confessed his adultery, was outwardly repentant. The members were willing to take him back as their pastor, when he was ready…even though he had already resigned. I was quiet, distant. From Zach's attitude toward me I didn't think he was really sorry. He didn't seem broken and penitent.

Again we left Nick with the Lamb family next door and went away for a few days to gain equilibrium in our marriage. We drove north toward the Canadian border. Talking led to argument, so by the end of the first day we were mostly silent. Driving into a small town we noticed a movie theater. "Shall we go see a movie?" Zach asked.

"Sure," I answered. Maybe a distracting story would help lessen our misery.

The movie was a comedy with a triangle plot…a marriage being broken up by one partner playing around with someone else. The circumstances were too like our own. I began crying silently…Zach was laughing.

He kept laughing, and in my hurt I became desperate. I walked out of the theater, unlocked our car and took some money out of Zach's wallet in the glove compartment. I bundled up warmly with hat and gloves…my blue pea jacket was thick. I relocked the car. Zachary had his own key.

And I began walking south out of town. Crossing a creek, I considered jumping in…but the water looked bitterly cold. That would be a hard way to die. I kept walking south, out of town, beyond the lights into the darkness. It was cold, but not freezing. On and on, into the dark where the stars overhead shone brighter. There were so many of them! Multitudes of pinpricks of light, glowing, pulsing...and the Lord's presence was so real.

He was with me, comforting me. "It's going to be alright," He said.

A car hummed in the distance behind me. The sound got louder, the headlights brighter. I turned around and looked...it slowed, stopped. It was a four-wheel drive vehicle, with three men in it.

"Do you want a ride?" one asked.

I hesitated. "How far are you going?"

"Down to the next town—it's about ten miles away."

"Sure," I said. I jumped in. It was warm.

We rode a mile or so and I began to have second thoughts. These men were friendly, but I didn't know them. And what would I do in the next town? I really needed a ride all the way to Bagley.

"Just stop and let me out," I said suddenly.

"Are you sure? It's far out of town." They were unsure, curious about me.

"I'll be alright. Just let me out."

They stopped the car and I opened the door. "Bye...thanks a lot!"

They drove off, and I turned around, began walking toward the faint lights of the town I had come from. On and on, about an hour I walked. It was getting so cold.

When I reached our gold Maverick, Zach was in it with the engine running. It was 11:45, almost midnight. "I didn't know where you were," he said, bewildered. "I decided to stay till midnight and then head to Bagley. You only left me enough money for gas to get home!"

I had little to say. He seemed to be living on the surface of life, whereas I had been torn so deep the tectonic plates of my being had shifted. I was trying to find meaning, a new map for my existence. God was there, I could lean on Him, but where did Zach fit in? If he wasn't truly sorry for breaking our marriage vows, how could I exist with him?

We found a hotel, crawled into bed together. In the morning he held me close, wanted to be intimate. Was this a way to heal our marriage?

Would the fabric of our life grow together if the strands of lovemaking resumed? I made love with him, but the deep hurt remained.

Driving home, we picked Nick up, and I kissed, hugged him. Our precious eight month old baby whole, trusting. "God, keep him safe in this upheaval," I prayed silently.

We stayed a few more days at the parsonage deciding what to do. We had notified our parents about what had happened. Zach's parents were shocked and hurt...I could hardly imagine how my parents would take the news, coming in a letter. They would want to talk, to be with me, but there was no way they could come home now.

Our planned vacation to Arizona with a cycle ride up the coast of California seemed pointless since our relationship was so broken. My vision, my future story was so damaged I was losing hope. Zachary didn't want to be a mission worker now, and he didn't seem repentant for what he had done. What could I do?

One late afternoon I sat in the rocking chair in the living room, feeding Nick his bottle. Zach was off running errands. The shadows deepened as I looked out the curtained windows. I had a thought. Maybe he would be jolted into grief if I killed myself! He would see how much he had damaged me!

I laid Nick down in his crib in the bedroom, and found Zach's pistol. I began searching for bullets, but couldn't find them. I looked for several minutes...and then began to think more sanely. If I shot myself, that act would probably send me to Hell. I would be committing murder. Hell would be much worse than my pain now.

"God, help me," I cried.

I put the pistol away and started dinner. When Zach came home I shared my despairing thoughts. He didn't seem greatly moved. I wished my parents were here...they would really care, have a plan.

THE PHOTOGRAPH

We finally repacked our suitcases, said goodbye to church friends, and drove to Grandma and Grandpa Hofer's in St. Paul. Zach was going to work in construction with Grandpa for a few weeks while we got our bearings. We began to slip into a schedule until one evening Zachary didn't come home!

Grandma and Grandpa were also anxious about Zach...we all prayed. I slept restlessly that night. When he returned the next afternoon he seemed different.

"I went back to Myra, but I didn't sleep with her," Zach told me. "Then I went to the Daystar ministry center and got help. I'm sorry. I'm ready to work on our marriage now."

I was amazed and relieved, but in a few days Zach began to withdraw again. He didn't want to pray...he didn't really know what he wanted. We decided to drive to his parents in Arizona. Having already visited with Rev. Leo Bereth about the reason for Zach's resignation, our commitment to this Alliance district was over. Zach didn't want to counsel with Rev. Hall. I felt as if I were floating on an open sea with no moorings, no harbor in sight.

Through the long hours of driving to Phoenix Nick was cranky, and cried a lot, reflecting our tension and pain. Mom and Dad Noll were so glad to see us, and fed us well. They had fun with Nick, who was now crawling. I had long talks with Mom Noll, and suggested the four of us sit down and talk openly. I thought that perhaps Zach would really listen to his parents, take some admonition.

It didn't work. Zachary didn't want to share his heart, listen to my grievances, or their advice. He left the table angry and wouldn't talk.

We found a Christian marriage counselor, took personality tests, tried not to argue. "The tests show that your personalities are at opposite sides of the spectrum," the counselor informed us. The advice he gave didn't seem to help much.

One afternoon I curiously opened up Zach's wallet in our bedroom, examining its contents. I saw a photograph of Myra, and a letter from her. The picture was one I had taken in our parsonage living room with the new camera the Smith's had given last Christmas. Something snapped in me. I began to scream, to shout in anguish. Zach rushed in horrified, followed by his parents.

"How could you have her picture in your wallet!" I yelled. "I took this picture of Myra, and she gives it to you, and you keep it to remember her with! We're supposed to be rebuilding our marriage, and you're even writing to her! You're continuing to hurt our lives—not heal them!"

Zach apologized. "I know I'm confused...I think I love you both. I need time to get away, to be sure of what I want."

In a day or so he had a plan. "If you want to go back to Ebro, I'll go to Alaska for a month. If you want to stay here, I'll go back to Minnesota. I want a month apart to think through who I am and what I want to do.

I was in a quandry. I certainly didn't want him flying as far away as Alaska. It would be hard for me to travel back to Minnesota and live in the parsonage, with Myra down the hill. It would be much easier to stay here with the Nolls, but then Zach would be in Minnesota, closer to Myra. Wouldn't he be more tempted to go back to her?

"I'm not planning to go back to Myra," Zach affirmed as we discussed possibilities. "I just need time to be alone and think."

WALKING IN THE DARK

I chose to stay near the Nolls...but I wanted my own place. So we scouted around and found a small efficiency apartment in Phoenix, a 20 minute drive from Mom and Dad. The efficiencies were lined up behind the regular apartment buildings, which were clustered around a large pool. They were the Pharoah Apartments...and I decided later it was my spiritual time in Egypt.

When Zachary flew to Minnesota it was June...the days were long and blisteringly hot. Both Nicky and I had trouble sleeping at night, so I would stroll him in a nearby subdivision, up and down the long quiet streets where squares of yellow light shone onto the sidewalk. I imagined myself walking with Jesus.

"Lord, I'm so lonely, but you are here with me. You are my Husband, Nick's Father, and you love us. You really care. Please take care of Zach. Speak to him, show him truth. Help him to give his life back to you...bring him home."

The Lord was there, so real. He comforted me. I looked into the golden lights of the windows as I strolled by, and wondered when Nick and I would have a happy home again.

In the mornings I slept as late as Nick would allow me, fed him cereal, read the Bible. I began putting promises from scripture onto 3 by 5 inch cards, and reading them throughout the day when I needed strength.

"I will be glad and rejoice in thy mercy; for thou hast considered my trouble;

"Thou hast known my soul in adversities, and hast not shut me up into the hand of the enemy. Thou hast set my feet in a large room." Ps. 31:7, 8 (KJV)

"Yea, let none that wait on thee be ashamed; let them be ashamed who transgress without cause. Show me thy ways, O Lord; teach me thy paths. Lead me in thy truth and teach me; For thou art the God of my salvation; On thee do I wait all the day." Ps. 25:3-5 (KJV)

I decided to get out of the house in the late mornings and walk several blocks to a restaurant, where Nick and I shared breakfast. We walked the same sidewalks every day, so the neighborhood grew familiar, and the servers greeted Nick and me cheerfully. The eggs, toast, and hash browns were delicious. I tried to stay encouraged, to trust, to live in hope.

Often in the afternoons we would swim and splash in the pool. We were getting brown...and as Nick got chubbier, I lost weight. In the evenings I couldn't eat much—I had no appetite. Toward the end of July I was down to 103 pounds.

Every day I felt tension as I looked in the mailbox for a letter. Zach wrote only once in the four weeks that stretched into five. At times, getting desperate, I tried to telephone Bonnie to reach him. He called back once or twice, but seemed distant.

I was attending a charismatic church nearby on Sundays, so decided to seek counsel from a lady on staff. Paula was loving, sympathetic. "I went through pain like yours years ago," she told me. "I understand. The

Lord will get you through. Read Isaiah 54. It can be your chapter." And she prayed for me.

Later at the apartment I opened up to that section of scripture.

"For thy Maker is thy Husband; the Lord of hosts is his name; And thy Redeemer, the Holy One of Israel; The God of the whole earth shall he be called. For the Lord hath called thee like a woman forsaken and grieved in spirit, And a wife of youth , when thou wast refused, saith thy God. For a small moment have I forsaken thee, But with great mercies will I gather thee..." Isaiah 54: 5-7 (KJV)

Comforting words. I held tight to them, to Jesus, during those days.

I would visit Mom and Dad Smith often to talk and pray. And I loved to stroll Nick along the canal behind their house, especially at sunset. Sometimes during other long evenings I would put Nick in his car seat and we would drive out into the desert, watching the gold and rose and purple colors unfold as the sun set behind dark blue mountains. God's desert handiwork was so exquisite, with lacy bushes, saguaro cacti, and scrub oak scattered on desert sand. It seemed that in pain there was a deeper reception to beauty.

Occasionally during the hardest nights when I couldn't sleep I would call Leota. It was an hour later in Minnesota, but she would answer sleepily, listen carefully, and really pray. I received strength to go on day by day through her and others' prayers. Mom and Dad were beseeching God for Zach and me, I knew, as we wrote letters back and forth. And Isaiah 54 was my chapter:

"O thou afflicted, tossed with tempest and not comforted, Behold, I will lay thy stones with fair colors, and lay thy foundations with sapphires. And I will make thy windows of agates, and thy gates of carbuncles, and all thy borders of pleasant stones. And all thy children shall be taught of the Lord, and great shall be the peace of thy children. In righteousness shalt thou be established." Is. 54: 11-14a (KJV)

My friend Dawn Wheelock who I had lived with several summers ago (with her parents), was still in Phoenix, now married with a child. She tried to encourage me, babysat Nick. I tried to work a shift or two for a nursing agency while she watched Nick, but it was too stressful. I was barely keeping my nose above the water edge of life.

During this time I looked for helpful books at the library and in bookstores. Classics like Jane Eyre were a pleasant distraction, but one small book seemed written for me: Hinds Feet on High Places, by Hannah Hurnard. In this allegory Much Afraid is going to the High Places assisted by Sorrow and Suffering, her companions. She passed through a dry desert also...and in the end Sorrow and Suffering were turned into Grace and Glory.

The four weeks drifted into five. Nick turned one year old July 22nd, but we delayed celebrating until Zach arrived from Minnesota--he had a building project to finish.

When Zach flew in we celebrated at the Smiths with a few friends. Nick crawled and took tentative steps, delighting us all. He was cheerful and chubby, our burst of sunshine in struggling times.

Later at the apartment Zachary and I talked. "Yes, I want to work at the marriage now," he told me. "I know it's the best for all of us."

"I know you've been with Myra," I said. "You hardly wrote or called. Did you sleep with her?"

"Yes, once. But I'm done with her, and I want to try now."

I didn't know what to say. My wounds from Zach were beyond words. He didn't seem repentant. On what foundation would our marriage be rebuilt?

There was no intimacy between us. We had pleasant times with his parents and with Nick...and at the end of the week Zach had changed his mind. "I want a divorce," he blurted out one morning. "This is just not working. I'm not the same person I was before."

After all the weeks of waiting and prayer I had no argument left. I couldn't make him love me or serve God. I had to let him go.

"Alright," I said slowly. "I have to figure out what to do, where to live. I suppose you're going back to Myra."

"I don't know what I'm doing. I'll just take it a step at a time."

A SMALL HOME

Dawn Wheelock and her husband offered to care for Nick for a few weeks until I figured out where I would live. Mom Smith had muscular dystrophy and Dad worked fulltime, so they were unable to watch him alone. They were sorrowful about Zach's decision. Mom prayed for us often, but they didn't know how to help Zach and me. We hugged goodbye with tears.

I held Nick tight before handing him over to Dawn. "I'll come and get him as soon as I can," I told her.

"We'll take good care of him. Call whenever you can...tell us how you're doing, OK? The Smiths are going to help too."

Zachary and I headed east in the little Maverick and were quiet most of the way. I considered where I should live, praying silently. It was the beginning of August, and my parents weren't home on furlough until early next summer of the following year. I could live near Romaine in the Chicago area where she had a nursing job. Or near Grandma and Grandpa Hofer in St. Paul, who could help with Nick--or try to get my old job back in Fosston, and live near Leota and Bonnie, until Mom and Dad came to the States.

The first night we stayed in Woodland Park, Colorado. The next night we were somewhere in Kansas, in a nondescript hotel.

Lying next to Zach I was amazed and wondering. "This is our last night together. Three years of dating, almost five years of marriage...and this is our last night in the same bed." My emotions were numb in grief. I couldn't absorb this truth. I fell asleep.

By afternoon of the next day we were near Chicago. We found Romaine's apartment, and I hugged her long, wordlessly. Ro still had her long, golden hair, but didn't wear glasses--she had contacts, and looked beautiful. We took Zach to the bus station where he would ride north to St. Paul, where his Bronco was parked at Grandma and Grandpa's. "Where are you going to live?" I asked

"I don't know," he said quietly. "I suppose where I find work. In the Twin Cities or up north. I'll keep in touch." He kissed me lightly.

"Bye," he waved to Romaine and me, carrying his suitcase and bag.

It seemed unreal, what was happening. Was this really Zach? He had turned into someone I didn't know.

Romaine was deeply sympathetic. "God's going to take care of you, Marti. It's going to be OK."

We spent the next couple of days visiting, and I got reacquainted with Jim Webber, Ro's fiancée, a former missionary kid from Dalat High School. They were to be married next December at the church Jim's parents pastored. I was so happy for Romaine...but the Chicago area did not seem like the place I should live. I needed familiarity of location, since I was going through so many other changes.

Grandma and Grandpa in St. Paul welcomed me gladly. Zach had stopped by as he travelled on north. They were deeply saddened over the separation, and tried to be comforting. I considered staying in St. Paul, but nothing seemed quite right.

So I drove on north to Bagley, stayed with Leota and Josh...and they told me of a small house I could rent from them. "It was my parents' home when they were living," Leota said. It's on the edge of town, with pines around the yard.

We went to look at it the next day. Painted white with green trim, the little two-bedroom house looked inviting, with a big yard, and a gooseberry tree in front of the kitchen window. The living room was carpeted a warm gold, and the kitchen had room for a table and chairs. I liked it!

"Could I paint the bedrooms, maybe wallpaper the bathroom?"

"Sure. You can make it as cozy as you like!"

Driving west to Fosston Hospital I found I could get my old job back, working three evenings a week. Since I had reasonable rent I could work part time, if I was frugal. We had sold the big Harley motorcycle to pay bills, and Zach had agreed to make my car payment and insurance. God was making a way for me.

I heard that Zach had gone back to Myra again. I could accept this mentally, but emotionally it was unabsorbable. He was still my husband!

How could the ex-pastor go and live with his mistress in the town he had pastored? Was there no fear of God in him?

Leota offered to organize a moving day where she, Bonnie, and others would help pack and carry my belongings. I dreaded going to the parsonage myself. On moving day I was at my new home to receive furniture and boxes...and later we all gathered for dinner at Leota's house. Amazingly, Zachary came for dinner also, after moving out his part of the belongings. He was cheerful, genial, seemingly untouched by this splitting of our lives. Leota was kind to him. "He really doesn't know what he's doing, Marti," she said.

In the next couple of weeks I settled into the house and started work. I painted my small bedroom a soft pink, and Nick's light blue. Bonnie's friend Larry helped me hang book shelves on the long wall of the living room, and I found a shimmery gold couch from a used furniture store. Old-fashioned lamps cast a warm glow, and pictures on the wall made me feel welcome. One framed print was of the Marriage Supper of the Lamb. It reminded me that Jesus was my Husband here.

I had been talking to Dawn Wheelock on the phone, and Nick was doing well, she said. He'd had a few stitches on his cheek after falling from a swing, but it was healing. I was lonely for him, and praying for money to fly and pick him up. Living paycheck to paycheck it was hard to save much...should I ask the Smiths for money? I had no way to directly contact Zach, and I certainly didn't want to go to Myra's house.

On Sundays I attended the Ebro church where an older man named Clyde was now interim pastor. He was quiet, kind, and being of Ojibwe descent, he fit into the community well. I shared my prayer request for flight money one Sunday, and a family who farmed nearby came up to me later.

"We've received some tax return money lately," the man told me. "We want to give the tithe to you, so you can bring your son home."

I was overwhelmed. "Thank you so much!" I choked out. "This is such an answer to my prayers!"

In about a week I had several days off in a row so I could drive to the Twin Cities, fly to Phoenix, pick up Nick, and fly home.

It had been a month, and Nick didn't recognize me. He was calling Dawn "Mama." Hugging him close, I expressed my appreciation to Dave and Dawn for all their good care. "How can I thank you enough! I'm going to send you money later."

"We were glad to do it," Dawn answered. "We'll be praying for you all."

ROCKING CHAIR BY THE CHRISTMAS TREE

It was so comforting to have Nick with me in our little home. He toddled around smiling and energetic, pulled on my leather boots, climbed into the lower kitchen cupboards. Each night after his bath we would sit on the couch, read a simple Bible story, and I would pray for him, for us. He loved the story of the Good Shepherd finding the lamb. When we turned to the picture of the lamb with the Shepherd carrying it home on His shoulders, we would cheer together. I was surprised at how much a fifteen month old could understand.

Jean, a Christian single parent offered to babysit Nick during my evening shifts. Her children played with Nick...and when I picked him up at midnight he was ready to tuck into his crib. After he was asleep, I'd make a cup of tea and sit in bed with my Bible.

"Lord, I feel so alone. But your Word says that you meet those who look for you. So I will expect you to be here. I look for you, and even if I never see you, I know you are here."

I would read scripture, look up and talk, and listen. And occasionally I could see Jesus. He was there looking at me, patient, compassionate. In white, with long brown hair. Later I would put the Bible down and turn off the light, asking for there to be six angels: one at each edge of the property, and two by Nick and me. I had no doubt they were there.

While attending a women's Bible study that Leota had started, I made new friends. Priscilla and Loretta were also single parents who attended the church in Ebro, so we began visiting each other.

Slowly I was adjusting to my new life—a whole new paradigm. I worked best with long term vision, but in this season I was living week to week. When Zachary divorced me I could never be a fulltime missionary with the Alliance. Perhaps I could do mission work with another church organization? But right now I needed to survive until Mom and Dad arrived home—about six months away.

One day I decided to drive to Ebro and pray with Bonnie. I knew she lived right next to Myra, and Zachary was living there…but God could help me. I worshipped in my prayer language all the way into Ebro, past Dan's car in front of Myra's house, and carried Nick into Bonnie's cozy home. She hugged me. "Good to see you, Marti. How have you been?"

"I'm ready to pray together. I need strength to keep going."

We shared over coffee, then interceded at length. For our families, for Zach and Myra, for work for Buck. We praised and did spiritual warfare. I left strengthened, and kept praying all the way home. God's grace was enough for me! The Lord was my High Tower, my Victory.

Three evenings a week I drove the 18 miles from Bagley to Fosston to be charge nurse of the evening shift. The doctors and coworkers were kind and sympathetic--they knew of my separation from Zach. Once in awhile I confided in Dr. George, but he had no advice for me. How does one make a man come back to his family? Especially when he's enthralled with another woman. I knew only God could work on my behalf.

One evening another friend and I attended a charismatic Bible study in Bemidji led by some college guys. I asked for prayer at the end. Things had changed, and now Zach was working in St. Paul.

"Zach my husband and I are separated, and he works in the Twin Cities, but every weekend he comes home to live with this girlfriend. And each Saturday and Sunday I feel this tug at my heart, this grief that I can hardly bear."

"You need to cut a soul tie to Zach," the leader explained. "We have soul ties to many people, but between a husband and wife this connection is especially strong. When this is cut, you'll feel more freedom."

I began to pray, to cut the soul cord, but broke down weeping. I hurt so much!

"We need to pray first for the Lord to heal your heart," the leader said gently. He prayed for me, along with others, and inside I distinctly felt healing! In a few minutes I spoke out and broke this strong soul tie in

Jesus' name. Later, when I drove home I felt free, whole. I was married--but not broken over Zach. And I continued to pray for him to come back to the Lord.

The weeks rolled on. The leaves on the gooseberry tree outside the kitchen window turned gold and red, then fell off, leaving red berries that the birds would eat. Each morning I had a quiet time with the Lord, made a plan for the day to get out and have coffee, visit someone—unless I was going to work that afternoon. I tried to fight bitterness and depression everyday by controlling my thoughts and having a schedule. Mostly it worked.

Once in awhile Zach did stop over to see Nick, take him out for a few hours. It was hard to get emotionally back on track after that…and Nick would cry more often the next day or two. When Zach came sometimes I reasoned with him, tried to use charm…but nothing moved him toward me. He had started the divorce proceedings, but agreed to delay them until my parents came home in the early summer. They had written and requested that—they wanted to talk to him.

The hardest part of everyday was dinnertime--the time when men come home and hug family, sit down for a good meal. I decided we would dine with Jesus. When the food was on the table I sat down facing the window and the red berried tree outside, with Nick to my right in his highchair. At right angles was Jesus' place. I lit a candle to symbolize his Presence, and the loneliness lessened. Jesus dined with us every night. He filled the emptiness.

As the days grew colder I bought Nick and me new coats. I found a cranberry red jacket trimmed with fur on sale, and Nick a dark green one with a furred hood. We played in the snow, threw snowballs, took pictures.

It was December, and Christmas was coming. In between working I planned small gifts for friends, for Nick, mailed off packages to family. Zachary was now in Arizona, visiting his parents.

Jesus was the center, however. What could I give Jesus for Christmas? I talked to Him about it over tea, sitting in bed one night.

"Why don't you give Myra and her three girls my present?" He answered.

I considered. "Well, your Word says to love your enemies, and do good to those who despitefully use you. I've been praying for her. I would need your grace. At least Zach isn't there right now."

The Lord seemed pleased with my answer.

So a few days later I bought three dolls for the girls and a jewelry box for Myra. I wrapped them with paper and ribbons, and one evening drove to her small house. I knocked on the door shakily. Myra opened the door and light shone on the snow covered front step. She looked surprised.

"Hello...these gifts are for you all, from Jesus, Myra."

"Thank you." She was almost speechless. "Thanks a lot."

I handed them to her. "Merry Christmas!"

I drove off to pick up Nick, relieved, happy. The gifts were given to Jesus, in his name.

I could feel His pleasure. My cup of joy flowed over.

A friend from church cut small Christmas trees for Priscilla and me, and I decorated ours with Nick's help in the corner of the living room. "What a chasm of change from last year," I thought to myself. "In the parsonage Zach and I were spiritual leaders, happy with a new baby.

Now I'm a single parent, coping...glad that I have to work Christmas afternoon, so I won't feel so alone."

With the lights and ornaments the little tree looked both scraggly and winsome—a Charlie Brown type of tree. I had bought Nick a child's rocking chair to place by my own rocker near the tree for Christmas—but it was in a closet now.

Christmas Eve arrived and Nick and I feasted with Leota, Josh and others. It was a big table of friends and extended family, with some Scandinavian specialty dishes everyone raved about. I felt awkward...I so wanted to be near my parents. But I was thankful for good friends who loved me.

Hugging Leota goodbye I stopped at Priscilla's house and we exchanged gifts over tea and cookies. Finally I came home. What was Zach doing now? Did he miss me? If only I could drop in on my parents and share my heart with them in Irian Jaya. I put Nick to bed and prayed with him.

Finally I sat on the gold couch, with just the Christmas tree lights on. "I'm here, Lord. I know you see me, and you care. You are my Husband. I'm lonely, but I know you are enough."

I listened. His presence filled the room. Looking near the lighted tree, I saw that he was there. Sitting in the rocking chair next to the tree, looking at me. Regal and humble, Jesus…in white robes, with compassionate eyes. He understood. Everything would be alright.

He filled Christmas.

He was Christmas.

TWO STEPS FORWARD, ONE STEP BACK

During these months my stability was in Jesus, but I sometimes questioned him. "Why am I going through this pain, Lord? I've given my life to you, tried to obey your call to be a missionary nurse. I married a man who also felt called to missions. So why am I separated from Zach and stuck on a sandbar in my calling? It seems so unfair."

The Lord was patient and clear with me. He reminded me of times when I argued a lot with my dad in years past, and later with Dan. He showed me I had never learned real submission in the small circumstances of life. Now I could learn it, in these rocky times. He also reminded me of the moral impurity during my years of dating Dan. I had never committed fornication, but I had compromised sexually many times. "You sowed bad seed that you are now reaping. If you and Dan had stayed morally pure, he would have had a stronger will to resist temptation with Myra."

I acknowledged this. I had sown the wind, and now I was reaping the whirlwind.

Continuing to attend Leota's Bible study, I listened to some of the women's stories. Many of them shared how the Lord had shown them their "old nature"—how totally lost and depraved they were without God. I listened attentively, but couldn't identify with them. I had come to the Lord as a little girl. I knew I was a sinner, but had never seen how utterly corrupt my sinful nature was without Jesus.

Meditating on this one evening on my gold sofa, a veil was removed from my spirit. The Lord showed me my depraved old nature. Without Him my natural self was a cesspool. My only standing before God was Jesus' holiness given to me because I had repented.

In the past some had called me naïve. I had been rather innocent as to my own and others' predisposition to evil. I hadn't even believed Bonnie when she warned me about Dan and Myra. Now I could see more clearly how we cannot trust ourselves to do right, but wholly need the Lord, His Spirit's power to help us.

Though I sometimes walked with the Lord closely and had revelation, at other times I stumbled with blurry vision. A leader from the Christian and Missionary Alliance had called once, asking if I believed it would help if my parents came home from Irian Jaya.

"I would love to have them near me," I answered. "But I don't think it would change my circumstances. Zach wouldn't come back to me just because they were here. So don't bring them home for me."

Little did I realize how much I needed their wisdom to steady me. For three different periods in the year I lived alone in Bagley, I dated men. I was lonely, and rationalized that soon I would be divorced. I was compromising my spiritual life—and damaging God's cause. After each time of dating, the relationship would become heavy, uncomfortable...so I would break it off, and press deeper into prayer for Zach. Even though there was no adultery involved, it was wrong.

Some days were pierced with more pain than others. I was in the car at Bagley's only stoplight one day with Nick in his car seat when I noticed Dan walking across the street in front of me. He was holding Myra's hand. He noticed me, waved, and walked on.

That was my husband...the former pastor! How could he be so blatant, so uncaring?

After another incident I became angry. I had dropped Nick off at the babysitter's house, and was driving west to work. Nick had a fever, but I had to work...I couldn't afford to stay home with him. Nearing the car in front of me, I saw it was Zach's Bronco, with Myra sitting close in the front seat. I began crying out to the Lord.

"God, you see me. I'm seeking you, trying to serve you, to be obedient. And I'm struggling, hurting. They look happy. God, I'm one of your children. I'm yours. I pray you defend me! I can't defend myself, but you can! Do something!"

Two visits broke up the long winter months—the first was Jim and Romaine's wedding after Christmas. I left Nick with Grandpa and Grandma Hofer in St. Paul and rode with another bridesmaid to the Chicago area. Romaine was radiant as all of us bridesmaids walked slowly down the aisle in red velvet trimmed dresses, holding lighted candles. Uncle Dewey gave Romaine away and Jim's dad presided over the ceremony...and Mom and Dad shared and prayed by tape recording.

So special, meaningful, but Mom and Dad were again missing a wedding. Such a cost they were paying for the gospel to reach Irian Jaya!

The second visit was from Uncle Dewey in late spring. I picked him up from the small Bemidji airport and he saw my house, the church and the empty parsonage in Ebro. He took a picture of me holding chubby Nick outside the church. My long blond hair was beribboned in two ponytails, and I looked happy. But in reality I was barely keeping afloat, with my nose above the waterline of distress.

We visited Bonnie and her family down the road, past Myra's house. Bonnie kept in touch with Myra, trying to encourage her to come back to the Lord. She gave little hope to Uncle Dewey for our marriage. Later he found Zach and talked to him.

That evening he told me, "It doesn't look encouraging, Marlene. But I can see that you're doing well, and we are praying for you."

"Thank you, Uncle Dewey. We'll come through this...Mom and Dad will be here this summer, and the Lord is with me!"

Winter stretched on and on. I began working nights. The shifts were quieter, the nursing assistants older than me, and very helpful. Zach was now living in a rented house across the tracks in Ebro, but still seeing Myra. Sometimes he babysat Nick at night from his house, then I dropped him off at Jean's so I could sleep, and picked Nick up again in the late afternoon. So on some days Nick stayed in three houses.

Bonnie and I met for coffee at her home sometimes, and prayed together. One time she seemed troubled. "I have news, Marti. Myra's at a cancer treatment center. She has cancer of the cervix. She's getting cobalt therapy."

I sat down in a chair. "She has cancer?"

"Yes. And she's had two miscarriages…one not long ago. Both Zach's babies. The second one was five months along."

I was at a loss for words.

"I want to visit Myra, but Buck needs the car for work. Could you give me a ride to the clinic tomorrow? It's a long drive."

"Sure. I'm off tomorrow."

Bonnie and another of her friends rode with me on the long drive to the clinic. I prayed as the others went into Myra's room. "Such strange circumstances," I thought to myself. "Like a soap opera. I can hardly believe I'm living through this." I prayed for Myra, but felt little compassion. I was just glad I hadn't found out about the pregnancies earlier. Was God defending me? Would Zach want to come back to me someday? Driving home we were all sober.

The gooseberry tree in the front yard leafed green, and grass sprouted where snow had been. It was wonderful to take bike rides to visit friends, with Nick in the seat behind me. Later I rode the small motorcycle Zach and I had bought months ago, with Nick in front holding onto the handlebars, travelling slowly.

In the summer Mom and Dad, Dan and David arrived home via the west coast, visiting Romaine and Jim in California where they were now stationed. Our reunion was so sweet. Dan was now 18, had graduated from Dalat High School, and David was 16. They were young men, taller than me. Dad now had an Amish beard and looked wise, with smiling eyes. Mom looked the most worn. My struggles had exacerbated anxiety…she had trouble sleeping at night.

They saw my little home and later talked to Zach. He was still adamant that he didn't want to reunite, and at this time he had money to finalize the divorce. Our separation had been about a year now. They accepted his decision and in a few days I hugged them goodbye. Mom suggested, "Maybe you can move down near us now, Marlene, and live near us in St. Paul."

"That's a good idea, Mom. When the marriage is over."

Some days later I received a call to come to the lawyer's office and sign divorce papers. Walking in, I signed my name in the right places and walked out numb. Was this how a marriage ended?

So much money and effort went into an engagement, marriage, furnishing a home, having children. Years of interactions with family and friends.

There should be a ceremony required to divorce someone, I decided. The one divorcing should have to invite all of the former wedding guests, stand in front of them, and explain why they weren't going to keep their vows. How could anyone break a covenant quietly when it damages the spouse, children, and extended family so deeply? Now I understood experientially why it says in Malachi that God hates divorce.

In a few weeks I felt ready to move to the Twin Cities. With the divorce final and Zach bent on staying with Myra I was totally letting go. It had taken months for my emotions to absorb the fact that Zach really didn't want me. And I believed that scripturally I was free to remarry.

I visited Mom and Dad in their apartment in Roseville, a suburb of St. Paul, and applied to work in surgery at the Samaritan Hospital where I had worked before.

"I want to hire you," the nursing supervisor told me, "but the charge nurse in OR just went home ill an hour ago. She needs to interview you also. Could you come back tomorrow and see her?"

"I'd be glad to," I replied, and we set a time.

I had decided to also check out openings at Swedish Hospital. The hospital had enlarged, and was now renamed Metropolitan Medical Center (MMC). I drove to downtown Minneapolis, applied and interviewed the same afternoon…and was promptly hired! "You're a Swedish grad," the nursing supervisor told me. "It's good that you want to come back here and work."

So…I cancelled the appointment I had at Samaritan, and started searching for an apartment near my family. Finding an upstairs one bedroom in Roseville, I asked the caretaker if she knew of a good babysitter. "I do childcare. Your boy is two years old? I can take another child. I live just downstairs from you."

I was amazed at how quickly everything fell into place. "Thank you, Lord…thank you that you are leading me."

After friends had a farewell for me, Mom and Dad and my brothers helped me move, fitting boxes and furniture into a U-Haul trailer. Later Dad hung a long shelf above the rocking chair in my new apartment, and even formed a bookshelf with stained boards and sturdy bricks. Gauzy curtains, artful pictures, the gold sofa. The oak table and Nick's high chair squeezed into the kitchen. And in the bedroom a small bed for Nick across from my double bed. I was home! Carvings from Indonesia, rose colored lamps, and Nick's toy chest. Personal, complete. And my parents were a few miles away.

I was rich. With the Lord and my family I was rich.

Marti Anderson

Bliss and Sue Bowman surrounded by Sue Carol, Inez, Evans, O'Neil and Christine.

The Bowman Clan with Marlene and Romaine.

Teenagers! Gordon and Duane Larson

Gordon and Peggy O'Neil court in Washington, D.C.

An early morning breakfast at Nyack Bible College.

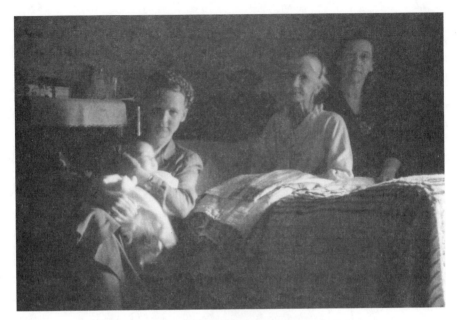

Marlene with Mom, Grandma and Great-Grandma Bowman

Pastoring in Wilmore, KY with their first-born.

Heading to the mission field on a Dutch freighter.

The Larson family farewell in New York City.

Trekking out from Homejo station.

Sturdy carriers for Romaine and me.

Precarious bridges!

Playmates John and Cathy with Rosalie Fenton and Leona St. John.

Airstrip finished in the Ilaga Valley.

A happy reunion!

The Danis, a warlike tribe.

The bark house-barely finished.

Romaine and I with Dani girlfriends.

David and Danny- Danis at heart.

Mom was placed in Pneumende Kom's clan-He was my "Uncle."

Dani men decorated themselves more than Dani women...

Sunday church gatherings.

Discussions followed at the end of service.

© Gordon F. Larson

A feast of sugarcane.

Eventually worship services were held around the valley.

I loved trekking to them!

Danis are more surefooted…

Birthday celebration!

At Base G with Miss Heikkenen and Betty Johnson, Marlene, Bev and Barton Boggs, Romaine, Larry Lake.

Visiting down valley before leaving for Dalat High School and the States.

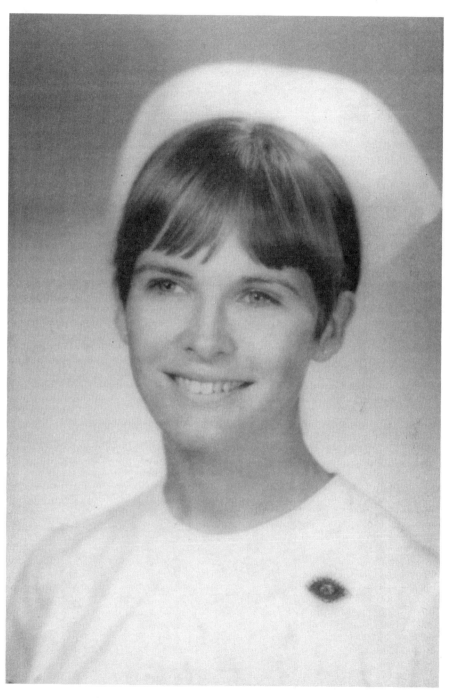

Graduation from Swedish Hospital School of Nursing!

Ebro Community Church with the parsonage in the foreground.

Leota, Bonnie and Priscilla with her daughter – praying friends.

Married at Soul's Harbor, in Minneapolis - May 2, 1975

At Valley Fair with Nick and Rhonda.

Beginning the journey with Larry Anderson!

Some leaders in the single parent ministry.

In the Ilaga Valley again...

Sugarcane break on the trail...

A sibling reunion on Pillsbury Ave.

Romaine and me at the Minnesota State Fair!

Big brother Nick, holding Jared.

Jared is one year old!

The Larson Clan – at David and Shellayne's wedding!

Cold winter in Elk River Minnesota!

Christmas gatherings…

Youth With A Mission outreach to Penang, Malaysia

Penang Beaches.

Dressing like Malays.

Having devotions with Krison.

Romaine and Jim visit from Thailand, with Cindy, Jimmy, Mike and Kelly.

An early discipleship training school with Tom Davidson the leader.

Handing the leadership over to S.H. and Emily.

Among the Dani tribe again with Jared!

Dad translating greetings to the Dani Tribe.

Feasting with the tribe.

Loving on the tribe.

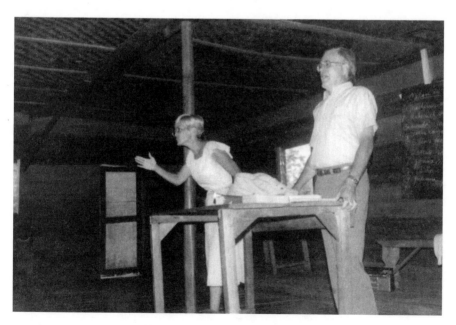

Teaching in the Eromaga Church.

Ken and Patty Freeman, now neighbors in Limon, Colorado.

Bob and Christopher Beard, prayer warriors with us.

Foxy, Jared's horse.

Our house on Scott Road, the eastern plains.

Sending Nick off to Oral Roberts University!

In Pattaya, Thailand – A gathering of workers sent out from YWAM Honolulu.
(Danny Lehmann is sitting in the middle.)

A frosty Colorado winter.

Staying warm by the fire with Karen, Larry's niece.

Writing papers…

Our doctoral class… Dr. Mayton (Far right, back row.)

Passing out New Testaments (Injils) in Turkey.

Our team at Ephesus.

Our apartment in Goa, India.

Teaching for Prabha and Mary in Lonavala, India.

A DTS class in Bangalore.

Mom and Dad, retired from Irian Jaya, (Papua) Indonesia.

Nick and Stacey with Hudson, Macy and Madeline.

Jared and Megan with Everett, Beckett, Francie, Lyla, John and Christine.

Climbing Mt. Sinai

Marti Anderson

...and still climbing!

REBUILDING WITH GOD

KITCHEN TABLE PRAYER

The alarm jangled, and I opened my eyes. Five fifteen am—still dark. But I was slowly getting used to the day shift at MMC.

Nick was sleepy as I dressed him and carried him downstairs to the babysitter. I kissed him goodbye sadly. I saw him so little when I worked fulltime, but he did have other kids to play with at Lori's.

Sunrise was still glimmering onto the windows of tall buildings as I sped west on the freeway to Minneapolis. Soon I was changing into blue scrubs and pulling a bright patterned cap over my hair.

Peggy greeted me at the nurses' station. "We're assigned to the same room, scrubbing together," she said smiling. "A hysterectomy."

"Great." Peggy was fun to be with—quick at surgery, friendly with the doctors. And she was a Christian.

We scrubbed in together, gowned and gloved, then covered the patient with sterile drapes before the doctor incised. Then there were two more cases to scrub for, and by the end of the shift I was picking packs for surgeries the next day. With three floors of surgical suites, MMC was a busy place.

Later, when I carried Nick upstairs from the babysitter I was tired and ready for a nap. But Nick was lively and talkative, so we took a walk down the street and looked for bunnies. And after supper he played in the bathtub as I washed dishes. Bible story and prayer together, a blessing on his head as I tucked him in. Then I settled onto the sofa and reflected.

How long could I sustain this schedule? I barely caught up on sleep on the weekends, and my paychecks were hardly covering expenses.

On Saturday I dropped in at my parents' apartment. Two year old Nick began playing with Tonka cars on the kitchen floor, lining them up in a long row. I sat with Mom and Dad at the kitchen table, sipped tea and shared my heart.

"You know, I'm just making it financially. And sometimes I'm so lonely...I feel more vulnerable here in the Twin Cities. I'm trying to find a church that has a singles group, that will help me grow. But I need you now. Do you think you could stay in the States another year?"

David was in the living room watching a football game. "Oh no, Marlene," he blurted out. "I don't want to stay in the States any longer than I have to. I miss Dalat, and I want to graduate from there!"

Mom and Dad looked sympathetically at me, then at David. "Well, Danny will be here, a freshman at Bethel College," Mom said slowly. "He could help you some."

I nodded. "That would encourage me. But I'm thinking more of a spiritual covering, and emotional security. I don't want to slide backwards spiritually."

"Let's pray about this," Dad said. "He has a plan for all of us, one that would work well."

"Let's ask the Lord to send me a husband before you leave," I suggested. "Then David can graduate from Dalat, and your work can still go on in Irian Jaya."

So we all bowed our heads. "Lord, you see our predicament," Dad said. "We're leaving for the Ilaga Valley, and Marlene needs a good Christian husband to take care of her and Nick. We're asking you to send one before we leave in June. A good provider."

"Yes, one who will really love Marlene," Mom added.

"One who will love you God, more than me," I added.

A few days later Peggy and I were again at the large sinks, scrubbing in for surgery.

"How are you lately?" Peggy asked.

"Well, I've been lonely. I'm busy enough with work and my son, but I need good friends. I'm looking for a single parent group that meets at a church somewhere.

"There's one that just started at my church Souls Harbor," Peggy exclaimed. There's this guy Larry Anderson who began a Sunday school class for singles. Larry's wife left him about seven years ago and he prayed for her to come back, but she remarried about five years ago. He has a daughter named Rhonda who lives with her mom."

"Amazing."

"In fact, I'm going over to the church after work. I could take you to meet him, if you want. Our church just bought this old Nicollet Hotel in downtown Minneapolis, and since Larry's a builder he's working there to renovate the rooms. We're going to use the old hotel also as a senior citizen residence."

After work Peggy and I walked into the dining room of Souls Harbor. I waited and sipped tea as she went to find Larry. I was in jeans, and my hair was in two ponytails, with ribbons. I was curious and nervous.

Peggy and Larry appeared across the large room, and I took a deep breath. This man was rugged, sandy haired, of medium height, and spray painted white like a ghostly cowboy. "Someone I could love," I thought to myself. He was a stranger, yet somehow familiar.

Peggy introduced us and Larry told me over coffee about the class. "It's to help single parents grow in their faith. We've all been through tough times, and this group is to keep our focus on the Lord, where our help really comes from."

I was struck by Larry's genuine warmth. Larry told me later he was struck by my youthfulness. "With those ponytails you looked about 17 years old."

I drove home slightly dazed. How could I meet someone who was committed to God and so handsome—so soon?

I began driving to downtown Minneapolis on Sundays to attend Larry's class and then the large church service. In 1974 Souls Harbor had around 2,000 in attendance, with multiple Sunday school classes for children and adults. The worship was excellent, the sermons fiery and strong with Rev. Gordon Peterson, a nationally known evangelist.

This singles class started small. Larry led well, but an older lady taught on biblical prophecy, and it didn't seem practical to my needs. In a few weeks Mrs. Prophecy became ill, and Larry was forced to teach. He was tentative at first, starting in Philippians and covering a few verses each week with discussion at the end. But his practical teaching on rejoicing in our sufferings was applicable, and the class began to grow.

One Sunday after class Larry and I kept talking. We wandered into church and sat together. After the sermon Gordon Peterson Jr. had us all stand, then hold hands in agreement while he prayed the benediction. Larry took my hand. It was strong, comforting. And afterwards he asked, "Would you like to go out to lunch together?"

"That'd be great. I'll pick up Nick from Sunday school."

The restaurant was subdued, elegant. "Lord, help Nick not to be rowdy," I prayed silently, as I fed him ice chips and crackers before the meal arrived.

"I have a daughter named Rhonda," Larry shared. "She's nine years old, and I often have her on weekends. I'm living at the church now, but I have a townhouse south in Bloomington. I'll have to show it to you sometime."

"I'd like to see it. My apartment in Roseville is a few miles from my parents. It's so good to be near them, now that they're back from the mission field. Growing up, I felt called to be a missionary nurse, but it's hard to imagine how that would work out now."

"I'm interested in missions also. I visited the Wycliffe training center in Colombia a few years ago. And did mission work in Alaska."

"Really!" I exclaimed. I worked in Homer and the Aleutians with a mission one summer, when I was married to Zach."

One weekend Zachary drove down from Ebro to the Twin Cities to see Nick. He took him out to see his grandparents, and when he brought him back we visited a little. "I want you to know I'm getting to know a guy, and it could turn serious. If there's any way you want to get back together, you should let me know now. I felt the Lord wanted me to give you this chance. If I remarry, Nick will be raised by someone else who will be 'Dad.' You would be more like an uncle, because you won't get to see him so much.

Zach paused thoughtfully. "Thanks for letting me know. No, I'm not interested in getting back together." He hugged Nick and kissed him. "Goodbye," he said huskily.

I began to see Larry more often. Every conversation with him was easy, open. We both had been hurt in our marriages, and now wanted to serve God wholeheartedly. He asked me to go skiing, but because of the bitter cold we ended up talking by a blazing fire at the ski lodge. Another night we shared on and on at Uncle John's Pancake House. His tanned face glowed under sandy hair, as we discussed missions, prayer, his boyhood on the farm, and the single parent group.

One night I invited Larry to dinner and served him pork chops with gravy and potatoes. He loved the dinner. And then he proposed…with me on his lap by the kitchen table, after Nick was in bed. He wrote it out on a sheet of paper, "Will you marry me, Marti?"

"Yes," I said, looking into his blue eyes. "I will marry you." We kissed, and then I drew back. "We haven't known each other very long, you know. This is a big decision."

"That's true, but we're older—and hopefully wiser--now. I'm 34, and you're 27. We're both committed to God, and want to live for Him and do missions. I'll ask your parents for permission…and I want you to meet my parents out in Monticello. They will love you.

Dad was now on a preaching tour with Alliance churches and wouldn't be back for several weeks. So Larry wrote him a letter, asking for my hand. Meanwhile we visited his parent's home. They were in their 80's, old enough to be my grandparents. Larry was the youngest of nine, and some of his siblings there that day were my parents' age. The family gathering was quiet, special, down home--I felt appreciated and welcomed by all who came.

"I've been alone for seven years," Larry told me later. "The family is so glad I'm dating a good Christian girl. And one who was raised on the mission field, at that."

My dad answered Larry's letter with his permission, and we celebrated when he arrived home. Then we met with our pastor Rev. Gordon Peterson, and his son Gordon Jr., who agreed to marry us. The date was set for May 2, 1975.

Larry and I saw each other every weekend, and during the week talked late on the phone. I was exhilarated and exhausted from lack of sleep. I was getting married! How was it possible that God was giving me so much joy after those long months of pain?

Our challenge was to keep the wedding simple and the bills paid. I found a long ivory dress with a laced bodice and high collar in back.

Romaine would be my matron of honor, another friend a bridesmaid…and we would all carry bouquets of gold and white daisies.

The main banquet hall at Souls Harbor was candlelit, and this time Dad walked me down the aisle. Having my parents here was so meaningful. For me the highlight was when we said our vows— traditional ones, slowly repeated after the pastor. Ones that would last till one of us went to Heaven.

Jacque and Brian Lother sang, new friends who were on staff. And as Gordon Peterson Jr. officiated I felt lovingly placed into a new enlarged family--Larry's clan and his church. Then Nick was dedicated to the Lord, and nine year old Rhonda received a blessing. She was shy and pretty with dark hair, in a long white dress.

"How can we be so happy?" I exclaimed as we drove to our downtown hotel. "I hope Nick will cooperate with Mom and Dad these next five days. They're not used to watching him that long."

"You and I are one now." Larry hugged me as I sat close to him. "We have five whole days to enjoy each other after all the busyness of life!"

"Even if we can't afford the ocean beach honeymoon right now, we can enjoy driving up north!" I laughed.

"Someday we'll go to the beach. We'll have a whole lifetime together."

BEAMS OF CEDAR AND RAFTERS OF FIR

Life slowed down for me after the honeymoon. Larry and I had decided I wouldn't work in nursing. I would stay home with Nick, and we would live on his salary. I loved the three bedroom townhouse that Larry's nephew Dennis had decorated. It was a 25 minute drive south set midst open fields, in Bloomington. We settled in my furniture and I made unbleached muslin curtains for our bedroom, hung pictures.

We had Mom and Dad and Danny for dinner one last time before they returned to Irian Jaya. David had already left for Dalat High School, and Romaine was down in Chicago with Jim. "Your new home is beautiful, Marlene," Mom said. I like the painting on the wall above the stereo. What kind of wallpaper is that?"

"Grasscloth, Mom. I like it too. I'm sure going to miss you when you leave in June."

"Yes, we're going to miss you," Dad said. "Especially now that Nick is growing so fast. Our first grandchild...and now Romaine will have another soon!"

"I'd love to come out and visit you all sometime with Larry and Nick. It would be so amazing to show them what the Ilaga is like, and our house among the Danis." I sighed. "Some day!"

"We'll pray it can happen," Dad answered.

"Well, if the Lord can bring you to Larry so quickly, He can certainly bring you to the Ilaga to visit," Mom smiled.

"We want this marriage to last," Larry said thoughtfully one evening after dinner. "So we should pray together every day. Spend time in intercession. I used to pray with Jerry my good friend for hours some evenings. Prayer will bind us together, move the Kingdom forward."

"Yeah," I agreed. "I was reading in the Bible lately about 'the beams of our house are cedar, and our rafters of fir,' wondering what that meant—maybe godly principles and practices. We can have devotions with Nick, then pray later when he's in bed. Also, it's important to me that we share the day together when you come home. We can sit and visit while supper is cooking. I felt that good communication was missing in my first marriage. Sometimes we just didn't understand each other. We need to take time to listen from the heart. Every day."

So each evening when Larry arrived home we sat on the couch and shared the day. Usually I had much more to talk about, and Larry would listen attentively.

"How did your day go?" I would then ask. He would have to think. "Well, besides painting and my lunch, not much happened." He would smile as I slowly drew details out with questions.

"I never learned to talk about my life so much."

"Well, in my family we talked all the time at the dinner table. Mom and Dad would have long discussions alone, too."

Later that summer we attended Basic Life Principles, taught by Bill Gothard. Larry had attended several times, but much was new to me. The seminar emphasized the power of a clean conscience, scripture memorization, principles for training your children, and how <u>not</u> to allow a root of bitterness to develop.

So now, in addition to our private devotions, Larry and I worked on memorizing verses in the evenings, and I repeated them with Nick each morning after breakfast. It only took five to ten minutes, starting always with the first verse, and adding on. We memorized about two verses a week and moved from Proverbs chapter one to two…and on slowly through three, four, five, until we reached, "let her breasts satisfy you at all times!" We halted then, laughing, and began to memorize Psalms.

After moving from a simple Bible storybook with pictures for Nick to one with more words, I decided to tear the first book apart and frame some Frances Hook drawings. I hung them in his room: Samuel listening for God's voice, Moses in the basket waiting for the princess to find him, David the shepherd boy who praised God as he watched the sheep.

Visually, audibly we wanted our new home to be filled with God's glory. We eventually carried the TV to the closet, and agreed to only listen to Christian music or classical. "Are we being too narrow, do you think?" I asked Larry one day.

"Well, we know what it is to struggle through pain and stay close to God. We're just keeping out distracting influences. We get news through radio and newspaper. And we are reaching out to help others through this single parent group.

We watched Nick grow more secure and less hyperactive through regular routine and Larry's consistent discipline. Every Saturday night was our fun family night for bike rides, games, popcorn, or stories. Like when I was a small girl in Homejo, with my parents.

At the single parent Sunday school class I began to teach with Larry. We prayed consistently for the members, and I began to telephone some each week. Our group became good friends and began to eat out together Sunday nights after church. Lucy was one of the most faithful—direct, outspoken, she had a way of putting the class at ease when she shared her needs and how God was answering prayer for her and her kids. In I Corinthinas 12, members of the church are likened to parts of the human body. I decided Lucy must be the adrenalin gland in our church body...with her openness life surged and flowed. Calm, dark haired Julie began to come faithfully. She had a strong, beautiful voice--she used to sing in nightclubs. Now she was an accountant, raising two teenagers. Ken Peterson and Ken Freeman, Chuck Melena, and Ty Story. Patty and Debbie, both fervent for the Lord, training their children.

When Pat Gasparac offered her home for a Friday night Bible study, we became even more of a family. "The Group," we called ourselves. Sunday mornings we covered principles in the New Testament, and Friday nights began going through the Old Testament. At first ten chapters a week, then we slowed down to two chapters for more in depth study. And Friday night was date night for Larry and me. We ate out and discussed what we would each teach, then enjoyed The Group, with dessert at the end.

We began to all sit together in the church services, celebrate Thanksgiving and Easter together. We were a large family, an organ in Christ's Body at Souls Harbor. Hurting members who had been healed, who were helping others.

One evening two years later we met at our townhouse for a meal with some of the leaders. It was July 7, 1977. We sat round our living room after the meal, sharing. "This date of 7-7-77 only happens once in a hundred years," I remarked. It must be a momentous occasion for this group.

"Yes, and there are twelve of us," Lucy added.

We all prayed awhile for the ministry, the church, our lives. "I feel impressed that like Jesus' disciples, we'll be eventually sent out two by two," I said. "We should make a covenant that as the Lord uses us, we're joined for life, committed to Him and each other."

"Yes Lord," Ken Freeman prayed out. "We are yours. Use all of us in this group for your glory, and as we covenant, may we always be united in your purposes."

We parted that night with a deeper sense of God's presence upon us.

HOME TO MY TRIBE

My new life was joyful and fulfilling, but my longing to be a missionary was always present. When would we live overseas? Where was my tribe? When Rev. Peterson asked people to come to the front of the church Sunday nights I sometimes went forward, knelt, and poured out my heart to God with tears.

"I will send you," the Lord would speak in my heart. "Just be patient."

One day I expressed my longing to Larry. "It would mean so much to have us all visit my folks, to have you and Nick see the Dani tribe. But it costs so much to fly."

"Well, we could put our townhouse up for sale. Since houses have been built around us the value has increased. We could take part of the profit and travel around the world."

"That would be amazing. Why don't we pray that if the Lord wants this he would just send a buyer! God could do that."

And so we prayed...and a week or two later I received a call from a realtor. "I have a client, a widow who is looking for a home in your area. Are you interested in selling your home and relocating?"

"Why yes," I answered, surprised. My husband and I were just discussing the possibility of selling."

After showing the house and agreeing on a price, we closed, storing our belongings with relatives. That September we flew west to Irian Jaya, with Ken Peterson leading the single parent group for ten weeks.

We landed in Bali rumpled and jet lagged. And I awoke in the early dawn to the raucous calls of tropical birds in the hotel garden. The tropics. I sat quietly on the balcony watching the day brighten with vivid color, listening to the birds answer one another. It was like being back in Sentani, being given my childhood world back...I was in grateful wonder.

We rented motorbikes and explored some of the island, Nick riding behind Larry. Then a few days later we landed in Biak, on to Sentani, and hugged Mom and Dad, laughing with joy.

"I can't believe we're all here." I exclaimed. "Sentani airport is so much more modern."

Dad grinned. "We're much more advanced and civilized now. More cars, electricity, buildings. You'll have to see Jayapura."

"Nicky, you've grown so much," Mom said, hugging him. "I can hardly believe you're six."

Sentani School now had over 100 kids, with more dorms and a dining hall. Even a swimming pool that Samaritans Purse had donated. And Jayapura was a small metropolis. Only Base G Beach looked the same, with rusting World War II tankers still lined up near waving palm trees.

The flight into the Ilaga Valley was what brought tears to my eyes. I was truly home again! The deep valley loomed wider as we descended slowly, circling. Across its breadth I could see large tin roofs with sunlight flashing off of them. "Those must be all the churches across the valley," I told Larry. "So wonderful."

We bounced up the grassy strip and it was almost like I was nine years old again, landing at my new home in the Ilaga. Only now there were fewer Danis to greet us, and some wore clothes instead of gourds or grass skirts. But they whooped and shouted like before, and after the plane took off we all sat in a group at the edge of the airstrip. Dad translated our greetings to them, their welcomes to us. As Larry was expressing his appreciation, he began weeping. "All of these churches across the valley," he told them. "You are following Jesus, and I get to see the years of God's work here." He wiped his eyes.

"Look," my dad interjected in Dani. "Larry is crying, and his name means weeping, 'Le adi,' in your language. See, that's his name."

"Aiah...ti abed o," the Danis responded. "So true. And here is Larson and Peggy's grandson. What is his name?"

"Nicholas...Nicky," Dad answered.

"We greet you Nikki," an old man said, shaking his hand Dani style.

"Say 'Kayonak,' Nick," I urged him.

"Kayonak, kayonak," he laughed.

The next two weeks were filled with Mom's delicious meals, in my beloved Ilaga home. We slept in my old bedroom, and in the afternoons looked out of the window at gray windswept sheets of rain approaching, like a silk skirts whispering up the valley. Then the rain pounded deafeningly on the tin roof.

Nick ran around the compound with other Dani boys, practicing on a small set of bow and arrows, and nearly killed one of Grandma's chickens. And we enjoyed a pig feast welcoming us in a nearby village, with steamed pork, greens, sweet potatoes, and kom (taro root).

One Sunday evening there was a large gathering of around 1,000 at the large new church down the hill. The kerosene pump lamps shone above dark heads, men on one side, women on the other. Dad translated for Larry and me...I felt so privileged to teach the Word among these people—my tribe. While teaching I expressed my love and longing for them, how I had missed the Ilaga all these years. But now we were together, and someday we would all be in Heaven together. I could tell the Danis were moved...many remembered me from childhood. We were one family.

Danny my brother was also in the valley for a few months, so one evening we sat in a large men's house and he taped conversation and Dani singing. The resonant sing-song of tribal voices praising the Lord moved me deeply. I would remember this evening forever.

After more days on the coast we hugged goodbye with tears, and took off, heading west. Biak, Ujung Pandang, Jakarta, Karachi, New Dehli. We were in awe at the Taj Mahal in Agra. And Larry and Nick had dysentery...we were careful what we ate and drank afterward that.

On to Israel, the YMCA at Jerusalem, where I had stayed with my parents as a teenager. Renting a car, we visited the Temple Mount, Nazareth, the Sea of Galilee, Bethlehem, Jericho, showing them to Nick. And on to Rome, Paris, London...we were all getting tired of travel when we landed back in Minneapolis at the end of ten weeks. It seemed strange to sit in the service at Souls Harbor, and find it the same. So much had happened to us.

And where would we live now? We stayed a few weeks in a suite on the 12th floor at Souls Harbor, and began to lead the singles again. We prayed. Somehow we didn't feel it was time to launch out in missions yet. We did have a fresh burden to disciple some of the newer Christians in the Group. Rev. Peterson told us about four large homes the church owned in south Minneapolis. He said they might be available as discipleship homes.

We toured them and prayed. There were two large older homes, and two duplexes which had been recently decorated. The Lord gave us vision for community and discipleship. "Yes, we would like to rent them," we told Pastor Peterson. "Thanks for the opportunity."

Slowly we filled the large houses on Pillsbury Ave. There were three in a row, and one across the street. We moved into the lower level of one Victorian duplex, and Chuck and Lucy Melena, newly married from The Group moved into the upper level. As good friends they were going to assist us. Joanne Holley and Sharon Madigan each had three children…they would live next door in the other duplex. Ken Peterson, Ken Freeman, and Ty Story moved into the men's home on the corner, and Julie Barnes would lead the women's home across the street.

Our first community meeting was warm, lively. "You know there's three women settling into The Palace," Julie informed us. "That's what we decided to name our home across the street. And there's a new girl named Shirley who wants to move in and be discipled, with her four year old daughter. She's outgoing and fervent for the Lord."

"Sounds like a great candidate," Larry said.

Soon after we settled into our old fashioned apartment we had big news for Nick. "We're going to have a baby," I told Nick. "You'll be the big brother now."

"Will it be a boy or a girl?" he asked.

"I'm not sure…but somehow I think it's going to be a girl."

Larry and I wallpapered the middle bedroom in cream striped paper with roses, and spray painted a crib white. I nested and decorated, took walks with Nick to the donut shop, and rocked on the front porch swing. Larry worked hard every day downtown at a parking ramp project. We began to share teaching responsibilities equally.

"You know, I'm concerned for all these single parent kids who have no dads at home," I told Larry one day. "Maybe some of these men would be willing to mentor them, take the kids out once a week."

"Let's talk about it at the next leadership meeting," Larry answered.

Several men were willing to be assigned kids to mentor, to spiritually father them. And in these months we divided the large Friday night gathering into four smaller groups, with a man and woman paired to lead each. And slowly, as time passed couples began to date, get engaged, and eventually marry, with Souls Harbor pastors' blessings.

Romaine my sister came to visit us in August of 1979. Jim and she now had two kids Cindy and Jimmy, and we all went to the Minnesota State Fair. We took pictures of her and me under the state fair banner—I was large with child and laughing in my ruffled blouse. "All of this walking might make me go into labor, Romaine. Wouldn't that be special!"

"Well, it would be alright, because we all want to see the baby," Ro smiled. That night Larry took me to MMC (the old Swedish Hospital), and early the next morning on August 28 our child was born.

"It's a boy!" the doctor told Larry, as he laid him on my stomach. "A healthy boy."

"Great," Larry laughed.

I was dazed from pushing, and the forcep delivery. I gazed at the little wiry body on my chest, his face squinched up. "He looks like you, Honey! And here I thought I was having a girl."

Later Larry brought Nick to see his brother through the windowed nursery. He handed me flowers that he and Daddy had just bought. "Here, Mom," he said with a gap-toothed smile. "These are for you. What is the baby's name?"

"Jared, Honey. It means 'one who is coming.' Jared in the Old Testament—his name was telling others that One, Jesus is coming. Do you remember what your name means?"

"Victorious warrior."

"And that's what you are!"

Nick smiled. "I like it."

We brought Jared home to Pillsbury Ave., brimming with happiness. Life was like a roiling bright river, almost overreaching its banks, our lives were so full. We were abiding in the Lord. He had made us fruitful.

"I am actually planted, growing up in my tribe," I thought, as I rocked Jared one evening. "I fit in here. Larry and I are ministering to a unique people group--single parents. Because we've been through divorces also, these people trust and love us. And we love them—they're our closest friends. Thank you so much, God."

But there was no margin. Feedings, meals, devotions, meetings, church services, counseling. We loved it all, but even Larry was growing tired.

Months later when he was laid off work and drew unemployment we had some relief. Larry took the time to paint the big gray Victorian duplex fresh white and cream colors.

"How can we keep up this pace when you go back to work again," I asked, sipping coffee at our kitchen table. It like you're doing two full time jobs, between cement work and ministering to single parents."

"Well, you carry the load too."

"Yes, and now with a new baby I'm even busier, and we have so little quality time as a family. Is it time to get a place of our own? Let's pray about it."

"We don't have much for a down payment," Larry answered. "But if God makes a way, maybe we can find a small house in the country."

As I scoured the paper from day to day I found a building company that offered loans for first time homeowners. And because we lived in the inner city, and Larry had been laid off, we qualified. Better yet, Larry could build the home for the company, keeping the costs down. Amazingly…the two and a half acre available lots were in Elk River, near Larry's family in Monticello. It was a forty-five minute drive from Souls Harbor, but we would be near the Anderson Clan. And we would still be a part of the Group our close friends, at church.

THE ANDERSON ETHOS

The house Larry built was set among scattered small cedar trees in a sprawling subdivision between the towns of Elk River, Big Lake, and Monticello. I enjoyed watching the progress: digging the hole, pouring cement, framing, roofing, sheet rock and taping, electrical, plumbing. The contractor supplied materials quickly, so within six weeks the house was complete.

Our friends in the single parent community were moving too. Souls Harbor was selling the four houses where we lived. We continued to meet Friday nights in cell groups and in our large Sunday school class. But eventually we sat with Rev. Peterson and discussed the possibility of handing the ministry over to Chuck and Lucy Melena.

We had thoughts of church planting in Elk River. Ken and Debbie Peterson were moving on to lead a downtown mission, and Ken and Patty Freeman were being called to pastor a church in Limon, Colorado. The prophetic word from July 7, 77 was coming true—we were being sent out two by two.

After handing the single parent ministry to Chuch and Lucy Melena our lives slowed down. And I was so grateful. When Nick boarded the yellow bus for school in Elk River and Jared was busy with toys I would sit at the sliding glass door sipping coffee, and look over fields and houses to the horizon beyond. After five years of ministering almost daily to single parents I felt drained. The field of my life needed to lie fallow and rejuvenate.

Once a week Larry's sister Helen and I met for coffee at a bakery in Monticello. It was a privilege to be planted more deeply into the Anderson clan. Larry was the youngest of nine children, and several siblings lived nearby, as did many nieces and nephews.

Helen was quiet like her mother, pleasant, with a gift of hospitality. During the many gatherings she and her husband Glenn hosted I observed the Anderson ethos. There was an unspoken drive, a silent determination to live clean wholesome lives, to serve God faithfully with your gifts. It was a long term marathon mentality of sowing good seed that would eventually give harvests. Quiet, loving. What astonished me most was how nice they were to each other.

Unlike many families, they avoided volatile discussions over theology or politics. When I raised a contentious subject, trying to generate lively discussion, I had no takers. No one wanted to argue, to ruffle each other's feathers. Was this the Scandinavian way?

But the Anderson ancestors had been pioneers, coming from Norway and Sweden. Where was the old trail blazing spirit? Were there no vehement opinions? It seemed that most of them were now persevering settlers, maintaining their lot in life here on the plains of Minnesota.

During our five years in Elk River I did mostly fit in. I loved being settled in our own home a few miles from the farmhouse in Big Lake where Larry had been born. I loved the family and the security this clan gave me. But I became restless. I knew the Lord had future plans for us. When would we move out to take the land God had given us overseas? Where was my tribe?

Over a period of years I had come to understand that as a missionary kid (MK) I was also what sociologists call a third culture kid (TCK). My first culture was the American one I was born into. My second culture was the Moni, Dani, or boarding school culture I was living during my childhood, and the third was an interstitial culture or "gap" culture that fit in somewhere between the other two. It was the one shared by other MK's or global nomads where we related best to those who had grown up in many different settings. I read that a TCK would tend to have "superior diplomacy, flexibility, linguistic ability, patience and sophistication. On the down side, there's insecurity in relationships, unresolved grief stemming from constantly leaving friends throughout childhood, and rootlessness." (Notes from a Traveling Childhood, p. 57) No wonder I felt rather different.

During nurses training I had mostly stopped discussing my childhood with friends. In northern Minnesota while pastoring with Zach I was working with American Indians who were like a second culture to me. Even the single parent group was a subculture unto itself that I could relate to as a TCK. But now in Elk River I observed the monochromatic Minnesotan lifestyle and missed my roots, the exciting tribal, traveling life I once had.

No one in Elk River besides my husband seemed to truly understand who I was, and I couldn't fully submerge my life into Midwestern rural culture. It seemed so strange, so illogical, since I had adapted many times before. But now in Elk River, from 1980-1985 when I tried to relax and fit in, it never fully worked. My head kept popping above the waterline of Minnesotan settler gentility.

For a few months Larry and I had church in our home with some single parents and new neighbors, then attended a growing charismatic church in Elk River. Eventually we drove the 45 minutes back to Souls Harbor every Sunday and worshipped with old friends. When Chuck and Lucy moved on to other ministry, Larry and I began to lead the single parent Sunday school class once again.

Through these years I worked in nursing, Larry built houses, and we prayed for the nations in our family devotions. Nick chose China as his country, Jared chose Afghanistan.

I kept asking God, "When will we go overseas?"

"Be patient," the Lord would tell me. "Be patient."

Hard as it was to wait, I could see God was building up our family life. The boys thrived on country living. We cut and hauled wood to burn in our lower level fireplace. I read "The Long Winter" by Laura Ingalls Wilder by firelight when snow was falling and the temperature plunged below zero. The boys sledded and we threw snowballs.

During summers we hoed in our big garden then picked beans, tomatoes, and young potatoes. We canoed down the Elk River. We picked strawberries under hot sun at a farm and piled them onto big scoops of ice cream for dessert that night. Nick got a small motorcycle and gave Jared rides. We were rich in God, good work, and family.

And I was gaining deeper perspective on life. When I worked in St. Cloud delivering babies, and then at small Buffalo Hospital in the maternity unit, the newborns amazed me. What would each tiny life bring forth? Each small bundle had an eternal soul that could affect their world for good or evil. One child's dynamic impact was infinite! Mother Teresa was once a baby, as was Hudson Taylor. As was Hitler… and Stalin.

Pastor Peterson died suddenly of a heart attack, and his home going was momentous. Six hundred cars drove to the cemetery and we meditated on the impact of one life at his graveside. After Gordon Peterson passed on, his son took over the leadership of Souls Harbor. Larry and I talked to him and his wife Nancy about becoming mission workers.

One night we attended a "Night of Missions" that Youth with a Mission sponsored. One of the speakers Jeff Littleton prayed with us afterwards about taking a Crossroads Discipleship Training School and then joining the mission. This time when we asked the Lord about the opportunity, God answered "Yes." I was overjoyed.

We put our house on the market, and it eventually sold. But oddly, during the process I had second thoughts.

"It's not easy to let go of this pumpkin colored home, Larry. I love the weeping willow we planted and the chokecherry tree by the swing, and the way the drive curves up to the house. Is there any way we could keep the house, rent it out? Nick is 14 now, and Jared 7…we have roots here.

"I understand. But we need most of the profit to take the discipleship training school. The support we raise we'll be living on as we do missions. However, we could save three thousand for a deposit on another house someday."

"That would be encouraging," I said thoughtfully.

"I'm ready to go wherever God sends us overseas. You know though, I'm concerned about my mom," Larry said slowly. "Dad is now gone, and it will be hard for her to say goodbye to us. She's so frail at 89…she'll be afraid she won't see us again. I'm going to pray the Lord takes her before we go, if her work is done."

And so it happened. Mom Anderson passed quietly away on a Saturday, sitting in her chair at Helen and Glenn's home. The funeral was Tuesday, and after farewells we flew west to Kona, Hawaii for our Youth with a Mission Crossroads training.

Larry was 46 years old, and I was 39. Finally we were launching our journey into missions.

CROSSROADS IN KONA

Our three-month training with Youth with a Mission was an adventure in adaptation. These twelve weeks in Kona, Hawaii were focused on character building, to be followed by a two-month field assignment in Asia. Nick and Jared continued their schooling with other kids at the base.

In January of 1986, YWAM was concluding a year of celebrations marking its 25th anniversary. Loren and Darlene Cunningham had started the mission in 1961, launching young people into short and long term ministries around the world. The base at Kona was set on a hill, with a grand view of the blue ocean below. The old motel framed by palm trees had been renovated, and now new buildings surrounded it.

Our family registered and settled into an upstairs room with a loft, right next to Peter and Donna Jordan our school leaders. There were 83 adults in our class, ranging in age from early 30's to mid70's. Many like us were attending to prepare for mission work, while others wanted discipleship. Some pastors came for needed refreshment.

The first day we were welcomed with leis of fragrant flowers and sat in a large circle in our classroom, an open sided pavilion. We slowly got to know one another as tall white haired Peter Jordan asked us questions:

"Where were you living when you were twelve years old?"

"How was your house heated then?"

"Describe a time in your life when you felt close to God, warmed by his Spirit."

Each question took time for 83 people to answer—especially the last one.

We ate our lunch and dinner in the same pavilion area and were assigned work duties. Mine was to sweep the classroom area clear of leaves every afternoon, and set plates on the tables for dinner… Larry's was in maintenance and carpentry.

Each week a seasoned leader taught us scriptural principles, and we had small groups where we could discuss and pray together. There were books to read… a journal to keep. Often after supper we and the kids jogged down the hill to the town of Kailua and sat on a stone wall, watching the sun sink below the sea. The last flash of sunlight would shine a brilliant green—we would exclaim at the flash, and after ice cream trudge up the hill for homework and devotions.

I was amazed at Paul Hawkins' stories of planting a base in Denmark, hearing the voice of God day by day, and the Lord providing everything for the team. Derek Prince shared teachings and experiences of his life in Israel…Dean Sherman taught on spiritual warfare. We were challenged to pray specifically, live holy lives, to bind and resist the enemy in Jesus' name. Danny Lehmann was teaching on evangelism around the ninth week when I came to the edge, the end of my horizon in faith and vision.

"Larry, let's pray and ask God what is next for our family." We were sitting on our bed in the hotel room. "I've been asking and waiting, and now I need to know how to move forward any further. Are we supposed to go on outreach with this school to Asia? What does God have next?"

"Sure," Larry answered. "When we need direction and faith, the Lord will meet us."

So we prayed, asking God to reveal the next step He had. "And we bind the enemy from speaking," I added, "and die to what we want individually. We just want to hear from you, Lord."

After waiting several minutes I got the word, "evangelism."

"Well," he answered. I didn't get anything. But Danny Lehmann is teaching on that subject this week, and he heads up the Honolulu base where they have a School of Evangelism. Let's talk to him.

Danny was a blond, muscular guy, a surfer. A former drug addict, he was now a family man who loved to witness for Christ and teach others to do the same. "We'd love to have your family come to our school," he said when we shared our interest. "It starts in April, and after three months the outreach will be to plant a long term base in Asia."

"That sounds great," Larry responded.

"I'll have the school leader send you applications.

We said warm goodbyes to the staff and students after our graduation love feast. Most were heading to Asia for the two month outreach. We would eventually have our outreach with the School of Evangelism, planting the new base.

Tom Davidson met us at the Honolulu airport in a van. He was a dark haired young man staffing the SOE. "There's 16 young people in this school-- you're the only family," he said on the drive from the airport. "It's going to be an exciting training."

The Honolulu base was a former World War II army post set back in Manoah Valley's verdant hills. It indeed looked like a mission station with a number of Quonset huts and renovated buildings among palms and flowering trees. We were assigned two bedrooms and a bath at one end of a Quonset—there were about ten girls assigned to the other end. Our classroom and dining hall was the Tin Cathedral, a large open sided building where doves cooed among the surrounding trees.

The orientation proved that this was a school for young people. "What is your favorite ice cream?" Dan Eastep the leader asked as an ice breaker. "What toothpaste do you use?" After much laughter we merged into more substantive discussions.

The teachings were informative, dynamic. A theological basis for missions, some church history, principles of evangelism, church planting, cross-cultural adaptation. And we were able to apply what was taught in evangelism outreach into the community. Two to or three times a week we were dropped off to share our faith in downtown Honolulu, the university campus, the beaches, and some evenings in the red light district. We took Nick and Jared in the evenings, and I was amazed to hear fourteen year old Nick witnessing to prostitutes on street corners. Saturdays when we took a bus to the mall Nick would share his faith with whoever sat next to him.

"This school is affecting our whole family," I told Larry. "We're changed. I've never been so bold in sharing the gospel before."

"It's true," Larry answered. "Now we just need to keep praying more finances in. We have the school mostly paid for, but we need money for outreach. And the $750 a month we raised before leaving may not be enough to live on in Penang, Malaysia, where they're sending us."

Every Friday during the school there was an evening meeting in the Tin Cathedral, open to members of the community. We began to invite classmates and visitors to our room for popcorn afterwards, and got to know Taylor, captain of a cable ship moored in the harbor. He was vitally interested in missions. After visiting his ship one Saturday we ate out, discussing life and calling.

As the time for outreach got closer, my stress over finances increased. "How are we going to pay for tickets and live in Malaysia," I wondered to Larry. "The kids' tuition alone at Dalat School will be about $500 a month!"

"I don't know…but we can stay as long as the money lasts. Everyone will have roundtrip tickets—so we could just fly home, if we have to."

Two things happened in answer to our desperate prayers. Nick came in with the mail one afternoon, and there was a refund check from the IRS of $2,500. "See," God had a plan," Larry laughingly told me. "The tax return came in good time."

We hugged each other in joy, and thanked God as a family that night.

The second answer was even more breathtaking, and it came through our new friend Taylor.

We were sitting in the last service before outreach, when Taylor wrote a note and handed it to Larry.

"I read his note, and thought he was pledging $100 a month to us," Larry told me later. "But then I looked more closely and it was $1000 a month! When I questioned him, he was adamant. He said the Lord told him to pledge this amount every month."

"Amazing," I breathed. "Now we'll have $1,750 a month to live on in Malaysia. That's about what a family of four would need. But it's a huge amount for one single guy to give. I'm calling Mom and Dad tonight to tell them about this answer to prayer. They've been praying a lot for us. They'll be so excited."

PIONEERING IN PENANG

Twenty-five of us boarded the plane for outreach to Malaysia—the eighteen students, four school staff, plus our boys and Dan Eastep's newborn baby. After two long flights we debarked at the Singapore airport where lilting music and delicate orchids set an elegant atmosphere. Our school leaders decided we didn't need to change money yet…we would just go directly to waiting taxis with our many suitcases and boxes.

Because the Singapore Ywam base was crowded our team was assigned a newly rented apartment block of rooms furnished with sagging bunk beds. Meals would be a six block walk away. I woke the next morning exhausted, to the noise of a small rattling fan. Our family had slept in, so we missed breakfast.

After showering I said to Larry, "There are no towel bars in this bathroom. No wastebasket, either. The beds are awful, and our little fan is so rattly—it's almost broken!"

"I know," Larry answered. "They must have just rented this place, and haven't had time to fix it up."

"Well, I can see that young single people can manage on outreach like this. But when you send a family out it seems like there should be preparation. The Alliance mission I grew up in did things so differently. They planned, prepared."

"Mom, when are we going to eat?" Jared asked. "I'm getting really hungry."

"We have granola bars, Honey. Here—you and Nick each have one. I hope we can find a place to eat near here, Larry. I can't believe we weren't allowed to exchange money at the airport."

"I think they were trying to get us efficiently to the base," Larry explained.

"But they didn't give the right address to my taxi driver. If he hadn't been able to call one of the other taxis I don't know what Nick and I would have done. We would have been driving all over the city with our luggage, looking for the rest of the group."

The four of us wandered a block or two down a commercial street until we stumbled upon a money changers shop, and then thankfully into a teashop that sold sweet buns. With food in our stomachs Singapore seemed more pleasant.

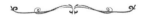

The next few days we had meals and some meetings at the main base, which occupied a whole story of a high apartment building. And we could explore the city, swim in the pool next to the base. Nick and Jared got acquainted there with Krison, a Singaporean 15 year old. He was friendly, open to the Gospel, happy to show us around the city. We met his mother, who sold chicken rice at an open air stall.

"My dad is in prison," he told us. "Mom supports me and my two younger brothers."

Before we left Singapore Krison asked Jesus to come into his life, and Larry baptized him and Jared one afternoon at the beach. (Nick had been baptized years earlier in northern Minnesota.)

He said goodbye to us before we boarded the train for Malaysia. "You'll have to visit us in Penang sometime, Krison," I told him. "We have your address. Write us back."

"I will," he said, brown eyes beaming. "Someday I will come."

Dan Eastep also saw us off. "We'll be less noticeable if we aren't too large of a group," he explained. "This way you can get settled in, since you have accommodations at Dalat School.

Malaysia's countryside was beautiful with green palm oil and rubber tree plantations, rice fields, and quaint Malay villages. We passed through Kuala Lumpur the capital, huge and bustling beneath the hot sun. More miles after the city of Ipoh we unloaded our many boxes and suitcases in Butterworth, and counted them. "Larry, one box is missing! It's the box of books and school notes—they're irreplaceable!"

"Oh no...are you sure?" We counted again. Same result. I began to weep. Finally we asked the station manager to call the Singapore station. Maybe we had left it behind.

After loading up into two taxis we crossed the ocean straits by ferry, then rode through Georgetown west around Penang Island into the residential suburb of Tanjong Bunga. Many buildings were old British colonial surrounded by tall branching trees, tropical greenery, and flowers. Blue green sea glittered in the distance.

The taxis stopped at Dalat International School, the same school I had attended as a teenager in Viet Nam! When the war forced them out, the CMA had relocated to the highlands of Malaysia, then to Tanjung Bunga. We were warmly greeted and settled into two well-furnished guest bedrooms that even had a kitchenette for tea and cookies.

"This is great, Mom," Nick exclaimed later. "There are a few kids still around this summer, so Jared and I can make friends before school starts. And there are basketball courts!"

"That's wonderful, Honey. I hear that Miss Kelck and Miss Wehr who instructed me in high school are still here. Wouldn't it be amazing if they taught you sometime!"

That evening we ate across the street at some Chinese food stalls. I looked around, observing different ethnic groups. We heard that about 50 percent of the population of Malaysia was of original Malay descent, many of them living in villages. They were the political leaders of the country. Their Malaysian language was similar to the Indonesian I had learned in Enarotali years ago. About 30 percent was Chinese--long term immigrants who became the commercial base of the country. And the rest—around 20 percent –were of Indian descent who had been servants when the British ruled. Now they had multiplied and prospered. It was legal to witness to the Chinese Buddhists or the Indian Hindus. But woe to the ones who tried to convert the Islamic Malays…they would be kicked out of the country, or possibly prosecuted.

The next day we wandered around the area looking for houses to rent. A block away there were new townhomes being finished that had small courtyards in front and back. And there was a furnished one for rent! Four bedrooms, three baths, with lots of marble flooring. In a few days, after negotiations, we were able to rent it for $300 a month. "Isn't this amazing, Larry! Such a cheap price, and so close to the school—and a short walk to the ocean."

"Well, the Malaysian recession is helping our exchange rate,"

"Maybe we could get bikes sometime?" Jared asked. "We could ride them to and from school. That would be fun." We were standing outside in our new home's courtyard near shrubs and small cedar trees. Jared's brown hair was wet at the edges with sweat, his blue eyes eager, sparkling."

"It would be great for you guys to have bikes," Larry assured him. You could get to school faster. We'll look around for some."

When the rest of the team arrived from Singapore a church nearby gave them barrack housing until Chiew Gim a young lively business woman took them to her well-furnished mansion. We began to have meetings as a team at her house, then go out witnessing two by two. Larry and I took the opportunity to shop for sheets, towels, and kitchen utensils, witnessing as we went. We found tracts and later small New Testaments in English, Mandarin, Malay, and Tamil, so my purse was heavy as we set out.

English was the trade language when Malaysia was a British colony, so most spoke it with a British-Malay accent. We learned that around four percent would call themselves Christians, whether Catholic or Protestant. Our team was like a group of friendly tourists...we engaged people in discussion, turning to religious topics as able. We met people at Monkey Park, Penang Hill, and down the coast at Batu Ferringhi where the tourist hotels were.

Some evenings we ate out at food stalls by the ocean, sitting on a stone wall. We chatted with families having their evening meal, watching the sunset. Many Malaysians were free thinkers—they enjoyed discussing religion and took our gospels with interest.

We continued to have team meetings and meals at Chiew Gim's elegant home. Cindy Kulwitzky was in charge of buying groceries, and she commented laughingly at one team meeting, "I bet I'm the only student on outreach who gets to go to market in a Mercedes Benz with a chauffeur!"

"We are blessed!" said Isabel, one of the team from Bolivia.

"Four of you are staying on with the Andersons to establish the base," Dan Eastep announced later. "Tom, Darren, Cindy, and Arlene. We should look for long term housing for you guys. And we need to be praying about a building to rent for the discipleship training school you'll start. And money for rent!"

Chiew Gim was standing by the kitchen door. "You four can keep living here until you rent buildings for the base," she offered.

"Wow," Cindy exclaimed. "Are you sure you want us that long?"

"Maybe we'll find a location right away," Darren Manzano the Hawaiian on the team said. "God can answer quickly."

After a farewell love feast at a restaurant and prayer commissioning we hugged the staff and rest of the students goodbye. Of the six adults who were staying, Tom was the only one who had staffed a DTS before. But God was with us.

Dr. Joy and Elsie who pastored large Full Gospel Assembly Church had been eager to have a Ywam base in Penang. Many of our team had been attending their church. Other enthusiastic supporters included Dr. Pauline and her brother Philip and his wife Florence. Our team began looking at large houses for rent. Rent was cheap due to the recession, but still we had to choose wisely. The Honolulu base was giving to us monthly for the first year, but their support wouldn't cover the rent.

Our team of six kept meeting to discuss and pray. Often I opened my eyes and observed each pair of feet. Clad in flip flops, sandals, or barefoot, each set were so individual. Long and thin, stubby and wide, with bumps and calluses. One guy had long toenails that needed cutting. How unique we all were-- each adding something that the others needed. Larry led, and I contributed with heart and passion. Optimistic Tom was an excellent administrator, and Cindy an effervescent women's discipler. Arlene was quiet and thoughtful, very organized as the base secretary. And Darren was diplomatic, loving others sacrificially.

One day we heard that Dr. Pauline and Philip had a large empty house we could rent. And it was fully furnished! We drove as a team to look. Off a busy street, it was two storied, L shaped, with huge spreading trees across the lawn. There was a large room for classes and meetings, good sized bedrooms for dorms, a furnished kitchen, and even a wood paneled air-conditioned room with a double bed in it. I remembered praying for a well-furnished speaker's bedroom. This went beyond my expectations! We were all in awe. And the rent was so reasonable.

We prayed and the Lord assured us this was the right location for our base and school. I remembered Paul Hawkins telling us in Crossroads how God provided for the new work in Denmark, years ago. The Lord was now doing the same for us.

After the four team members moved into the house we began praying for bunk beds, long tables for desks, some chairs, and God's timing for the school. Funds and materials began to come in. As the dates were set for the school we focused on praying for students, the right teachers, and how to get the word out. We printed an attractive brochure advertising the new school and mailed them to churches across Malaysia.

School began in November with eleven students...nine singles and a young couple with a child, SH and Emily. Since there was a large Ywam conference in Thailand around that time we incorporated the conference into the school schedule. All the staff and students took the train up to Bangkok, then southeast to Pattaya. The housing and grounds were rustic, the meetings anointed. And we were privileged to meet other Ywam workers serving in south east Asia. Kalafi Moala from Tonga led the meetings.

Back home in Penang various leaders brought good teachings in the succeeding weeks: Danny Lehmann, Frank Goebel, Matt Rawlins, local pastors, and even Larry and I. The students were in their late teens to early 30's. Everyone entered into intercession, work duties, and occasional street witnessing.

Before our three month visa expired, we took the train to Singapore to renew it. We had continued to pray for our box of books and notes...that God would somehow return them. So after getting off the train we checked with the station master. "No, there is no record of luggage left on that date," he said, turning pages in a worn notebook. An assistant went back to check in the storage room. He was gone a few minutes, then came back bearing a square cardboard box tied with twine.

"It's our books, Larry! The box we left on the platform! Thank you, Lord!"

"Well, no wonder they couldn't find it. There's no name on this box—nothing!"

"Thank you so much, sir. We are indeed grateful," I almost hugged him.

"Glad to be of service, Madam," the manager said, smiling.

Our few days in Singapore gave us and the boys time to shop and sightsee a little with Krison. He was attending church faithfully, he told us, and making friends. We found a Deli France and had chocolate croissants together.

A few days later we boarded the train for Malaysia. I was concerned we might not get three month visas again, but our passports were stamped with nary a question. Nick and Jared had yearlong student visas, so the official knew we had reason to live near our sons. He didn't ask our occupations.

Chugging north toward Penang I had time to reflect. "Lord, you're so gracious to us. I'm fulfilling my mission call, and Nick and Jared are attending the same Dalat School I did, and enjoying it. Thank you so much! What other good things are in store? Will Malaysia be our permanent home? You've led us to believe we won't live in Minnesota again. I would so like to know where home is."

This longing prayer of my heart continued through the following weeks of the DTS. It was around Christmastime when we renewed our visas again, this time in Hat Yai, Thailand.

Hat Yai was a frontier city filled with bars and brothels. We were saddened to see so many young girls being misused for money. One night after dinner we had devotions with the kids in our hotel room and prayed for the city. "Lord, you see all this human trafficking, so many people abusing others. You love these people. Help them. Send your truth to them, somehow," I prayed.

"God, help these people to want to do right," Jared agreed.

"Would you want us to come here after we establish the base in Penang?" Larry asked.

We waited on the Lord, listening, worshipping.

To my surprise, I began to get a picture, a map in my mind...of the state of Colorado. "I think the Lord wants us to pray for Colorado," I said.

We began to pray for the state, especially for Colorado Springs, where Larry's sister lived. Nick interposed, "I'm seeing a pennant, like for a football team. It says 'Colorado' on it.

"I see swimming trunks, and it has a tag on the pocket that says 'summer,'" Jared added.

Larry laughed. "This is amazing. I just saw a log house. You've prayed for a log home, Marti."

We kept worshipping, waiting on the Lord. "I believe the Lord is sending us to Colorado Springs, for it to be our home base." I concluded. "So unexpected."

"Well, our return tickets have to be used within a year," Larry said. "We could visit there this summer. If it still seems right, we'll move there after we finish our two year commitment to establish this base in Penang."

The DTS ended, with students and some staff going on outreach to Thailand. Larry and I began to speak in local churches some Sundays, both in Penang and on the mainland, driving the used car we had purchased. I loved taking the ferry across to Butterworth, driving down palm lined roads to small towns and teaching gospel truths to Chinese/Indian congregations.

That summer back in the States we checked out Colorado Springs, visiting Ken and Patty Freeman who were now pastoring in nearby Limon. We spoke in their church, later rode west and parked on a hill overlooking the Front Range. The blue mountains were majestic, stretching north and south of Colorado Springs. "I do have peace that this is where we should live after we leave Penang," Larry said.

"I do too," I answered. "I wonder why. I thought we would move to Thailand. Maybe it'll be a good home base for our kids, for us to go in and out of. Your sister and brother-in-law Dorie and Bill are here, so that's a blessing."

We flew back to Penang and rented a house further up the hill from Dalat School, next to friends from church, Ben and Ann Tan. And Ann began giving Jared piano lessons, which Miss Wehr my former teacher later continued. After buying a small keyboard, Jared's music began to fill our home. Simple songs with perfect timing!

Discipleship training schools continued, with the rest of the staff leading them. Larry and I prayed and decided to check out other Ywam bases in Asia where our DTS could go on outreach. Ann and Ben watched Nick and Jared for us, and we visited Pacific Islanders pioneering in Dhaka, Bangladesh. We flew on to Dan and Christine Bushy in Kathmandu, Nepal, and then to Calcutta where a leader named

Wendy showed us the work in the area. We were overwhelmed by the poverty in Calcutta. We visited Mother Teresa's compound, arriving when she was receiving visitors—I even got to shake her hand! From Calcutta we took trains to Hyderabad, then southeast to Chennai.

We landed back in Penang exhausted and amazed at the dedication, the sacrifice of God's people.

Nick was now fifteen, and Jared eight years old. We had continued regular family devotions and Bible memorization through the years, and both our boys loved the Lord. But in Nick's fifteenth year he began to get cocky and rebellious. One Saturday morning things came to a head. Our family outing to Georgetown was being ruined by his sullen attitude.

"Nick, there are some things we do as a family," Larry told him firmly. "You get to be with your friends during the week. Weekends are time for family. We're not going to have this afternoon ruined by your bad attitude."

"We have to pull together as a family," I added.

Nick nodded miserably.

"We're out here in Malaysia as a family team. If one of our own kids is thinking he doesn't want to serve the Lord, there's no use in us trying to disciple other Malaysians. Christianity has to work at home first. If we're failing you, why should we try to reach others? We should just move back to the States and stay there."

"I'm sorry," Nick said. "I do want to follow God. I'll try and cooperate."

Heavy rains were followed by a dry season. Some staff went home and other families moved to be associated with the Penang base as their children went to Dalat School. As the semester was ending we all prayed about who to pass leadership to. S.H. and Emily, the couple from the first school had proved faithful in tenacity and wisdom. We asked them, and after prayer they agree to lead the base.

At our farewell dinner we recounted God's faithfulness and laughed over memories. "Remember that Malaysian taxi driver you witnessed to so strongly that you made him angry?" Tom said to Larry. "It's a good thing you gave him a big tip...you might have ended up in jail!"

"Yeah," Larry laughed. "And remember when you were in the hospital with typhoid fever, Tom? You had us worried!"

"I was sick for quite awhile," Tom admitted. "I was concerned some of you would come down with typhoid. God has sure taken care of us all, even on all those outreaches to India and Nepal."

Goodbyes were sad but sweet. We trusted we would return in a year or two.

HOME ON THE RANGE

Adjustment to life back in the States proved difficult. It was like moving from nitty-gritty real life to Storybook Land. There were manicured lawns, beautiful houses, and elegant malls in Colorado Springs. Cleanliness, orderliness, wide streets and clean air. We knew we were living in the right city, but were not clear why we were living here. In Malaysia our purpose was well defined...here in Colorado we only knew we should find a good church, support ourselves, and eventually send Nick off to college. It was an in between time before returning to full time missions. And I felt a little guilty enjoying the good life in America.

We had spent our nest egg of $3,000 back in Penang...I had slowly relinquished that money toward the end of our stay there, with prayer. "Lord, that money was our down payment for another home. But we need to spend it toward rent and food and air tickets home. Give me your faith now, to move forward."

When we had arrived in Minneapolis Larry's brother Cy co-signed so we could buy a car. After visiting family we had driven west to Colorado Springs to Bill and Dorie's comfortable home. At the time there was no Ywam base here, and we didn't feel led to start one. We were looking for work, wondering how to rent a house. Bill and Dorie were warm and encouraging, but the late 1980's was a time of recession, and building was slow, so Larry did not readily find work.

One afternoon I had coffee alone after shopping for a needed light jacket at the Citadel Mall. I sipped my coffee slowly, observing well-dressed shoppers

"Lord, what are we to do? We have about $20 left, and Larry needs to find construction work. I need a good nursing job, and the boys need good schools."

"I am with you," the Lord reminded me."

"Yes, Lord. Thank you. But I feel poor right now. Please help me."

"I will," He told me.

Soon after, puzzle pieces began fitting into place. Bill and Dorie wanted to drive round the country in their RV and visit family. "Would you guys like to rent our home for a year?" Bill inquired. The rent will be reasonable."

"Sure," Larry answered. "We love your home, and this area is beautiful."

Larry began to find building jobs, and after applying at St. Frances Hospital I landed a full time night position in NICU with tiny newborns. In the fall Nick began eleventh grade at Doherty High School, and Jared the fourth grade at a nearby Christian school. God was answering our prayers!

Finding the right church took a little more time. For months we drove twenty miles north to Larkspur where Tim and Diane Ralph, old friends from Souls Harbor had started New Covenant Church. We loved their friendship, but the drive was long. Sunday nights we began attending another church on the west side of town—New Life—that had about 1,500 meeting in a strip mall. Ted Haggard was the young preacher, and Chris Hodges the worship leader/youth pastor who had just arrived in town. "We're going to have Bible clubs in the high schools," He told us. "Nick can help me begin one at Doherty."

The boys began attending New Life's youth groups, connecting with new friends. One named Christopher Beard became Nick's good friend and they started attending Tuesday night prayer at Chris Hodges home.

We settled into a routine of work, school, and church in Storybook Land America. "I still wonder why we're here," I murmured to Larry one night before we went to sleep. "This doesn't seem as spiritually needy a place as Malaysia. I can see it's great for our sons. They're flourishing in youth group, praying, witnessing. And I'm being used at the NICU with staff and babies, though I'm not proficient yet. But you've had to go twice to California for short building jobs. And we don't seem to have a real ministry."

"That's true," Larry sighed. "I don't understand it either. But we do have peace that we're in the right place. We need to keep praying."

"Well, if this is our home base for going out to missions, we should try to save and buy a home."

"Sure. It would be nice to be out in the country, like we were in Elk River. We could rent out the place when we go overseas again."

One day I found a newspaper ad that read: BANK OWNED HOME, split entry on 50 acres, 3 bedroom, 2 bath, unfinished basement, with barn. Needs work. $75,000.

I was excited. But walking around the property later with the realtor we were sobered. The barn looked ramshackle, with junk strewn around the yard. And the home needed lots of work, even though it was only about 10 years old. It seemed dark inside. Had there been occult activity in this house?

After walking the property several times and praying we finally felt peace to offer the $75,000. Our mortgage company made the bank do several improvements on the house, and during this process we kept saving for the down payment.

The day we closed on the house we were exuberant. We drove out to walk on the land. Our own home...on 50 whole acres! It had amazing views of the distant Front Range, and windblown meadows studded with prairie flowers. We even liked our Scott Road that blew dust when a car drove by. "Could I have a horse, Dad?" Jared asked, looking around. "We could all ride it."

"Well, there's plenty of grazing land." Larry answered. "We'll have to look around for one."

We cleared truckloads of junk from the farmyard, and hauled debris from the house. A wood ceiling for the kitchen, new counters, wallpaper, rich blue carpet, and a cleaning to the large moss rock fireplace. When we moved in at the end of the summer we had poured so much toil and sweat into the place it was truly ours. Each boy liked their bedroom…and we had the basement to finish.

In the fall Nick was a senior at Doherty High School, eventually driving his own car. He ran for class president, and though another better known classmate won, we were impressed with his outgoing confidence. Jared entered fifth grade at Peyton School, riding the bus with a mix of rancher and small town kids. We slowly absorbed the Midwest plains culture, even adapting to owning Foxy the chestnut horse who would not be caught to ride. She was so exasperating Jared eventually agreed we should give her away to someone more persistent.

Sunday morning and evening, and Wednesday night we drove long miles to New Life on the west side of Colorado Springs. The worship was dynamic, the preaching from Pastor Ted clear and powerful. The Lord sometimes used me in giving prophetic messages—Pastor Ted was very open in allowing the Holy Spirit to move freely.

And as we drove we went over our scriptures. We had begun with II Cor. 2:14 after Chris Hodges preached a sermon from that section of the Word:

> *"But thanks be to God, who always leads us in triumphal procession in Christ and through us spreads everywhere the fragrance of the knowledge of him…*
>
> *Such confidence as this is ours through Christ before God. Not that we are competent in ourselves to claim anything for ourselves, but our competence comes from God. He has made us competent as ministers of a new covenant—not of the letter, but of the Spirit; for the letter kills, but the Spirit gives life."*
>
> *(II Cor. 2:14, 3:4-6 NIV)*

We continued through chapters three, four, and on into chapter seven. The more we memorized the longer the recitation took, but we found as a family they became our verses, a part of our family DNA. We were living and breathing those truths.

Our passion for missions was translated into a Friday night prayer meeting at our house. Christopher's father Bob Beard and other prayer warriors joined us to intercede for our church and the nations. As friendships deepened we felt more at home on the plains. And music filled our house as Jared faithfully practiced the used piano we bought.

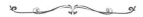

When Nick graduated we celebrated with a large open house. My parents arrived on furlough from Irian Jaya just in time. Older and worn looking, they still radiated joy. Even Nick's other dad Zach came, quiet and genial. "You've done a good job raising Nick," he told me, smiling. "He's a fine man. It's great to be at his graduation."

"Thanks," I said. "We're glad you could come. I know Nick is so happy to see you. We're planning on going back to Malaysia when he's in college."

That summer we began to send newsletters to raise support for our mission work in Penang. After settling Nick into the dorm at Oral Roberts University in Tulsa we drove to Minnesota to visit family and for Larry to do some construction work.

In December we celebrated an early Christmas with Nick and hugged him goodbye with tears. He would spend Christmas with Grandma and Grandpa Noll in Arizona. I was beginning to get feverish as we flew west from Los Angeles to Penang. I was also anxious about finances. We had only raised $350 a month in support. Leaning back in my airline seat I tried not to worry.

"Lord, Jared's Dalat tuition alone will be $250 a month. I thought you would provide enough support at the last minute, like you did last time. We don't have enough to live on, even if we stay at the Penang base. Please take care of us."

Peace slowly filled my heart. But my fever and nausea worsened as we flew west to Kuala Lumpur.

MONKEYS ON THE PORCH

I woke up the first night at the Youth with a Mission Penang base to the sound of frogs croaking in the lily padded sea marsh beyond our window. Their deep and discordant chorus droned on all night. A ceiling fan whirred above me, but I still felt sticky--and sick.

"How are you feeling, Honey," Larry asked, turning over.

"Better. I think the antibiotics from Dr. Pauline have lowered my temperature, but my insides ache."

"Try to get more sleep. Jared's sleeping in the guys' dorm for now. He's comfortable."

I'm glad we're safely here. But I'm worried about the future. How are we going to rent a house, buy a car, function here in Penang with so little support? Did we hear God wrong? Were we presumptuous in leaving with some savings but so little support?"

Larry squeezed my shoulder and spoke softly. "Well, last time the Lord did provide the $1000 a month pledge right as we were leaving. Maybe this time he has a different lesson for us. A steeper learning curve in faith."

In the following days Jared enrolled in seventh grade at Dalat School, reuniting with former classmates. As I felt better Larry and I wandered the seaside Tanjong Bunga area near the base and met new Ywam staff. Of our original team from Honolulu only Tom was here, returned from the States with Teresa, his lovely bride. SH and Emily the leaders had labored faithfully and now there were several new staff, including six Korean girls who were here to serve and improve their English. Jeff and Diane our friends from Kona, Hawaii had moved here to travel and teach in Asia.

Larry and I walked up the hill to the main road where small shops clustered. We found a teashop and ordered the strong Boh tea Malaysia is famous for. With cream and sugar, it was delicious. We sat outside where palm trees waved, and cars and rickshaws buzzed by. A hawker passed, carrying plastic dishes for sale on his shoulder. Cigarette smoke drifted behind us where older Indian men sat and sipped their tea. I slapped a fly that landed on my sugared donut.

"It's wonderful to be back, isn't it," Larry commented.

"Yeah. I feel like we belong here. Sort of like we've come home."

"But I wonder how we're going to fit in at the base. Our roles have changed."

"Well, you know my dream is to teach, whether in Malaysia or in other countries," I answered. "But our first goal should be to raise more support so we can stay here."

"Larry nodded. Tom is leading the DTS this fall. Maybe we can offer to staff it as well as teach a week or two. Later when we have more support we can travel out to teach in other nations."

After we mailed out around 130 newsletters our support began to slowly rise. Meanwhile Dr. Pauline offered to share her hillside mansion with us. She was an energetic Chinese Malaysian, brisk and efficient in her senior years, generous and hospitable. "You can use the bedroom and bath at the end of the house," she said. "It has a large veranda in front. And Jared can sleep downstairs where others have bedrooms. You can eat with us too, until you find a good house to rent."

"Thank you so much, Dr. Pauline. You are so gracious," I answered. "Would it be alright if we cooked on the front porch under the eaves? We can buy cupboards and a two burner stove. This way we can have family life with Jared more easily. And we can eat once in awhile with the whole family.

"Of course."

"And I can help with housecleaning sometimes, in the rest of the house."

This arrangement worked well for several months. We borrowed an old DTS van, cleaned it up, spraying ants out of its base. It had no air conditioning so we sweltered in the heat…but it was free!

As we staffed the DTS we got to know the Malaysian students. It was fun and challenging. The singles were young, with two student couples who were more mature. The first couple Dass and Rani were Malaysian Indians—he was an outgoing leader who had grown up on a rubber plantation, and she was trained as a teacher. The other couple Colin and Jo were college graduates, Brits who had been travelling the world. This time in Penang was for spiritual growth and direction.

Peter Jordan our former Crossroads leader came to teach at the school, and we hosted Peter for dinner on our veranda. "It's good to see you guys doing so well here," he said, leaning back in his chair. "And what a view of the harbor."

"Yes, we're really enjoying it," Larry answered.

"Except when the monkeys from the jungle next door climb up onto our cupboards," I laughed. "They're so cute, but one time they got into the flour and rice and made a mess! Exotic living does have its disadvantages."

We all laughed and had a wonderful evening of storytelling.

It was Jeff who found the empty home for us to rent on Haji Rafaie. A three bedroom, two bath home with cream colored floor tiles. The back yard was lined with greenery, the front yard faced a road and a hill from which loud Indian music floated down during the evenings.

Support had now risen to about $1,000 a month. We paid the first and last month's rent, cleaned and painted the house, scraping grease from the grillwork at the kitchen window. We dripped with sweat in the tropical heat, but the results were worth it. After buying bamboo living room furniture and curtains from a missionary couple who were moving back to the States, we sat in the living room and sipped lemonade. "It's beautiful," I exclaimed. "And I'm very thankful that Dr. Pauline offered her small piano for Jared."

Larry agreed. "You're getting so good, Jared it's even a joy to hear you practice."

"Thanks," he grinned. "I'm glad you made me keep practicing when I was younger, Dad. I love it now."

The Lord kept providing! We bought a car that had air conditioning, and began to use it for outreach. We visited with Bob and Kelly Parr, newer staff who worked with village people and hosted Ywam teams. As we visited Malaysian villagers our hearts were knit together in love and prayer for their work. We also enjoyed worshipping and serving at the

Full Gospel Assembly Church. I was sometimes used prophetically and one Sunday Larry and I taught. Sometimes we spoke in other churches, driving through small towns, jungles, and rice paddies on the mainland.

In the summer of 1992 we began to live on the edge again. Though we communicated faithfully with family and supporters we barely had enough income for food and living expenses. And I began to miss Nick more. It was expensive to call so we only telephoned him for 20 minutes every two weeks. He seemed to be doing well in classes and later with summer work, but he did miss us. "It's not like I wish you were here in Tulsa," he said. "But you're on the other side of the world. There's no one around if I really need something."

Nick's situation brought back painful memories from my college days. I felt we were neglecting him...like I had felt forsaken when my parents were on the field and I was in the States. I often left the phone crying, wondering why it was so hard. Did family always have to be apart for the Lord's work?

As Larry and I prayed together I asked, "Lord, why did I have to be alone those four years of college and nurses training? I was so lonely sometimes. I know the Danis needed the Gospel, but I was emotionally malnourished--like a plant low on nutrients--much of the time. I needed family. Father, are we doing the same thing to Nick?"

"Yes, Lord," Larry agreed. "Please show us your highest will for our family. Heal Marti's wounds from the past, and provide all Nick needs right now."

One day we received an unexpected letter—from the Internal Revenue Service! Larry tore the letter open. "They want to audit us," he said. "We've never been audited before. And our records are stored in Colorado. I have no idea how we could work with the IRS right now."

We answered their letter in handwriting, detailing our mission work and inability to provide records.

Our finances continued to be tight through the summer. As Jared turned 13 in August and entered eighth grade, his Dalat tuition was added to our monthly expenses. That fall semester Jared experienced painful sores in his mouth and throat. He had difficulty eating and began to lose weight, so Larry took milkshakes down to Dalat at noon to provide some nutrition. We kept praying.

Then one day Larry came home while I was fixing dinner with unexpected news. "S.H. and Emily are moving to Ipoh to pioneer a base."

"Really! He's the base leader and the national director. Why wouldn't someone else pioneer a new base there? Penang here is a larger city from which he can work."

"Well, he'll stay national director. But he wants me to take over the Penang base leadership. Are you interested in us doing that?"

I sat down at the dining room table, pondering. "My passion is for us to teach together, to travel in and out of Malaysia. If you're tied up with administrative work, how can we do that?"

"It would be more challenging. But we're the natural choice for this, having pioneered the base."

"That's true, but are we called to do it? God could use Tom in that capacity, or Jeff and Diane, if they wanted to take it on. Right now my focus is on getting enough support to live on."

We kept praying about the base leadership, and a few days later I finally had peace. "It's alright for you to lead," I told Larry. "In time we could travel and teach more after our support improves. But our finances are so tight now. We pray and pray, but I still worry."

"I know," Larry said. "It's not easy."

"So much of our emotional and spiritual energy is spent on just surviving financially. Is this God's best? In the Alliance mission my folks had their support provided, and they could just concentrate on mission work. Are we doing something wrong?"

"Let's just press on. Keep praying. God will come through. He's always faithful."

One lunchtime Larry came home after the base prayer meeting with news. He seemed both subdued and excited. I had stayed home recuperating from flu.

"They prayed over me today, installing me as base leader," Larry said soberly.

"Today? I had barely said 'yes' to God in my heart about this. I wanted to wait until our finances improved. I still hardly have faith to stay here, much less take on that responsibility with you. Why didn't they wait till I was there too?"

"I think S.H. just wanted to hand the leadership over."

"Couldn't you have asked them to wait till I could be there? We work as a team. Usually couples are prayed over together."

"I'm sorry," Larry answered. "I should have asked them to wait."

The process seemed wrong to me, but there was nothing I could do. In a few weeks the staff hosted a farewell dinner for S.H. and Emily before they left for Ipoh. Larry began to lead the base meetings and we started taking staff out for coffee to get to know them better and pray for their needs.

I decided the base needed decorating and there were funds in the base account for it. In the coming weeks the wicker furniture cushions were reupholstered, with new curtains that coordinated, and all the walls repainted in soft colors. I taped and Larry painted. We hung framed pictures and oriental wall hangings. "Don't you love the new look," I exclaimed to Kelly one morning.

"Yes. It lifts your spirits to have good decorating." We laughed together.

I kept praying and trying to trust the Lord, but continued to worry about our personal finances. I missed Nick and prayed that he wouldn't struggle. Jared was enjoying school and music. Larry was steady...he didn't seem to worry, he just hoped and prayed, on and on. As our rent came due we checked our dwindling bank account and discussed our options.

"Well, we can pay the rent and trust God for food for the rest of the month," Larry offered. "God's always been faithful."

"Or we can use our rental deposit as payment, and have plenty for food," I answered. "I feel like we're on the end of a limb, and it could crack off."

That week we received a telephone call from Dennis Stern, one of the New Life elders.

"There's news from your renters," he told Larry. "The well on your property has gone dry, and they're having water delivered by truck. A new well drilling will cost around $5,000-- I could oversee it for you. Think about it and call me in a day or two."

"Thanks, Dennis. I'll let you know," Larry answered.

That night Larry and I splurged and drove toward Batu Ferringhi to the seaside Lone Pine Restaurant. The antiquated eatery served reasonably priced food under feathery pines. You could hear the waves wash the beach and the wind whisper in the branches as candlelight flickered on the tables.

We sipped tea until the food was served. "What shall we do?" I asked Larry.

"Well, thank God the IRS cancelled their audit. But we don't have the money to drill a new well."

"Even if we borrow the money, it might take years to pay it back. We need a miracle."

"Well, we were sent out by New Life," Larry said, looking out at the waves. I suppose I should call Pastor Ted and explain our situation. We could stay or fly home depending on his advice."

Pastor Ted was hard to reach because he was suffering from inflammation of the vocal cords. He could only whisper. But Gayle his wife relayed his encouragement and told us the church would lend us the money to drill the well. We could pay it back as we were able. "Thank you," Larry told her. "We'll keep in touch."

In the coming days I shared with friends on staff about the dry well and our financial dilemma. I told them we were wondering if we should return to the States.

Jeff dropped in on us one day to advise us not to talk about returning home. "It's not helpful to the staff to hear you talk about leaving," he told me. "We can pray about your finances. But if you're struggling a lot here, perhaps you need counseling."

"I understand about not discouraging the staff," I answered. "But some are close friends, and they can pray with us. We're even told in scripture to bear one another's burdens. You know, Jeff, I didn't want Larry to take on the base leadership until our finances were stable. I agreed reluctantly."

"And I should have had Marti there when I was installed as base leader. She's felt left out," Larry added.

"Maybe you need counseling as you go through this," Jeff suggested.

"Right now we need more money for the rent and food—or I need a big gift of faith," I answered, crossing my arms. Jeff prayed with us and left.

A week later we decided to return to the States. No financial miracle happened…we used our last month's deposit to pay rent for the month, sold furniture, the car, and gave Dr. Pauline her small piano back. Tom Davidson was installed as base leader, and we hugged staff goodbye as we left for the airport. I felt bad that we were taking Jared out of school in the middle of his semester. "It's ok, Mom," he told me. "I have friends in Colorado." His blue eyes glowed under thick brown hair. "We'll be together with Nick soon, too."

"How are we ever going to catch up financially?" I murmured to Larry as we flew from Kuala Lumpur to Los Angeles. "We have to pay off the airline tickets and drill a new well. And since our place is rented, we have to find a small apartment for ourselves. Nick will have to hand back our car that he was using in college."

"I know," Larry sighed. "but God knows all about this. We're his children. He'll use this for good somehow."

WOUNDED BY A LEADER

Our return ticket was to Tulsa, Oklahoma. We hugged Nick joyfully. His blond hair was trimmed and his white shirt starched. "You've grown taller and look wiser," It told him.

"It's Jared who's changed the most," Nick said, ruffling his brown hair. "You're almost as tall as me now."

In the hotel and over meals we discussed Nick's classes and dorm life. He was an RA at Oral Roberts University, overseeing a dorm wing. He printed out excerpts from a book in his communications course on making five year goals.

"We'll read this," Larry told him. "It looks interesting since we're refocusing on long term plans now."

In a few days when we said goodbye standing next to our tan Chrysler Nick laughed. "Now I won't have a car, but you're closer to me in the States. And I'm so much richer with you here."

Back in Colorado Springs we quickly found work—Larry in various construction jobs and me at the Memorial Hospital NICU. We found a two-bedroom apartment in the Village Seven area, and Jared settled into 7th grade in a Baptist Christian school.

It seemed strange to be back in Storybook Land again, where the lawns were manicured, the streets wide, and the supermarkets big. I missed fulltime ministry, but it was good to begin paying off debts. The new well at our home in Peyton had cost only $3,500 to drill—less than the $5,000 we had expected.

New Life had grown to several thousand and moved into a new building in the open fields north of town. The worship was powerful, Pastor Ted's sermons instructive—his vocal cords were healing.

Nick came home for fall break and Christmas, and our family prayer times were sweet. We began to intercede at New Life Church Saturday nights in the main auditorium. Jared played on the grand piano and sang worship songs--some he had composed himself--as the rest of us walked around the large room praying. Nick went back to ORU and others joined us till we became a faithful band of Saturday night prayer warriors.

Larry and I continued to seek the Lord about future mission work and over several weeks formed five year goals. One was to build and sell houses till we could have one debt free. Then we could rent it out, helping support ourselves overseas.

"I'd like to live in the country again," I told Larry over dinner one night. "Watching sunsets, hearing coyotes howl at night, looking for Orion among the stars, without city lights."

"Maybe we should ask the Lord for a large piece of land where we could have cattle," Larry suggested. "We could raise them for six months at a time. Buy in the spring, sell in the fall, make more cash to support ourselves in missions."

"Well, you were raised on a farm…that might work!" I smiled. "Then we could travel overseas six months of the year when the cattle were sold. What do you think, Jared?"

"Country sounds fine with me. In five years I'll be a senior in high school, almost ready for college. So I wouldn't be travelling out with you, unless it was in the summers."

"Well, I'm going to start watching 'land for sale' in the Gazette," I decided. "The renters' lease is up late this summer. They've shown interest in buying our house on the 50 acres."

"Yes," Larry agreed. "And if we make enough money on that house we might be able to pay for land. In this slow economy land prices are often cheap."

"Remember that prayer time in Thailand when we got direction to come to Colorado Springs, Larry? You saw a log house. Maybe you can build one on the land!" I exclaimed.

"Boy, that would be a dream come true for you, Mom," Jared chuckled.

One afternoon when Larry came home from work I showed him a Gazette ad. "Look at this! There's 160 acres for sale northwest of Calhan for $40,000! It even has a pond. That would be about a 30 minute drive east of here."

"Amazing. Well, we'd better go and look at it."

We wandered over the rolling property the next day, astonished at how spreading it was. Off Ramah Rd., it was fenced with a row of trees near the ruins of the homestead, and a small pond to the west. Behind the trees there was a rise where our log home could be built and from there you could see the Front Range stretching deep blue beyond green fields, far in the distance.

"Wow," Jared exclaimed. "This place is huge. You could have a lot of cattle, Dad."

"I guess we need to be careful what we dream for. God can answer way beyond what we can ask or think!" Larry laughed.

We negotiated a contract to sell the Scott Rd. home to the renters and juggled the date for buying the 160 acres. Due to delays we ended up paying $42,000 for the Ramah Road land, but it was still a bargain price.

One Saturday we picnicked with friends on the hill where the log home would be built. "Can you believe these views, Dennis!" Larry exclaimed to our friend."

"God's sure been good to you guys," Dennis declared. "Almost a year ago you were squeezed over drilling a new well...and now you've bought 160 acres!"

"It's beyond understanding," I murmured. "I pray we can be fruitful in missions through using this place."

Through the fall and winter Larry built the log home on our hill above the pond, and I worked twelve hour night shifts at Memorial Hospital with sick newborns. We kept praying with our Saturday night prayer group at the church for missions and the church services.

In the spring we heard that a Youth with a Missions team headed by Karl Strand was moving to Colorado Springs. Karl was tall and friendly, a visionary who drew missions minded people to him. We met the team and formed friendships, having them over for dinner.

During Nick's spring break we picked him up in Tulsa and drove to Minnesota to visit family and our single parent group friends. While we were there Nick told us more about Stacey Matulla, who he was dating. Her parents pastored in Hastings... she was dark haired, beautiful, majoring in music, and loved the Lord.

"When I was praying you'd come back from Malaysia, it was partly because I wanted you to confirm any choice I was making in a marriage partner."

"Wow, Nick," I chuckled. "Was that why we struggled so much in the last months in Penang? Was God just answering your prayers!"

We dropped Nick off at the Matulla's home so he could catch a ride back to ORU with Stacey and her sister. During the short visit we were impressed with the family.

When the log home was finished and we moved in—it was like a dream come true. The logs were stained brown, with a red metal roof, and a long front porch over which two dormer windows shone in the dark like friendly eyes. I hung cream colored curtains against the wood walls and some landscape pictures.

How could all this stretching prairie be ours? The nearest neighbors Tony and Lou were a mile away, cattle ranching. We had panoramas of rolling meadows clothed with grasses and soap weed, of Calhan eight miles southeast, and the mountains far west. The almost half mile of driveway was uphill and muddy in the spring, so the car got spattered as I drove home from my night shifts, but our home on the prairie was worth it.

We continued to develop our friendship with Karl and his Ywam team. When Larry and Gary his nephew partnered to build a home on five acres in the country, they offered it to Karl at a discount to help his team. Karl was grateful, and when the house was finished many of the team moved in—singles and one family. Occasionally we met with the group, praying with them for the Crossroads school they were going to begin in the fall.

Then one day Karl asked us, "Would you guys like to lead the Crossroads school we'll be starting? You have missions vision and experience…I think it'd be a good fit."

We were surprised and excited. Would God want us to do missions from our home in the States? We had never considered that.

"Thanks for your confidence, Karl," Larry answered. We'll think and pray about this."

For three weeks we mulled over the opportunity, praying every evening as a family. "We'd have to raise quite a bit of support," Larry said by the fireplace one evening. "Not many people like to support missionaries who live in their own country and have their own homes."

"True. But it's a great challenge right here in Colorado Springs, to raise up workers for missions. Maybe we could each work a day a week in building and nursing to supplement pledged support. Just volunteer four days a week at the base."

"We could suggest that to Karl," Larry answered.

At the end of three weeks we had peace to join the Ywam team, and offered Karl our commitment, with the stipulation we be allowed to work a day a week to earn money.

"Sure," he answered. "I don't see why that wouldn't work."

I was elated, enthusiastic. Driving home with Larry I reflected, "It's so amazing the Lord would bring us to the States, give us a home, and allow us to work in missions with Karl and the team."

"Yes," Larry said. "But it may not be easy to raise enough support. We struggled to raise enough when we worked in Malaysia…how many people will want to pledge when we're right here in our home town?"

"Yeah. I would want to give to someone overseas, myself. It sure is a walk of faith, isn't it?"

We attended the Ywam team meetings intermittently, being busy with work. Around six weeks later Karl said he would like to attend our Saturday night prayer at New Life. He joined us as Jared was playing worship music up front, and we all walked, prayed, worshipped around the large auditorium.

At the end he suggested the three of us go up to see Pastor Ted who was in his office. We were surprised. Karl seemed a little nervous.

Pastor Ted was cheerful and friendly. Karl explained that he had brought us in because he had gotten three references on us since we were to lead the Crossroads, and none of them were really positive. He had another couple in mind who were joining their base, and he would like them to lead the Crossroad…we could assist them.

I was shocked. "Karl, you asked us to lead your school, and you didn't even ask us to apply. You didn't tell us you were getting references."

"What was negative in those references, Karl?" Larry asked.

"The one from S.H. said he wouldn't want to make you a base leader in Penang again, and the one from Jeff suggested Marti needed counseling."

"Well, we left Penang suddenly, that's for sure," Larry responded. "S.H. probably didn't understand that."

"And Jeff didn't like it that I was telling the staff we might return home if there wasn't financial breakthrough," I added.

After more discussion Pastor Ted concluded, "Well, Karl, you can choose who you want to lead your school. It's your decision."

"And we'll be praying about what we should do, Karl," Larry said firmly. "We'll be in touch."

In the following weeks I swung between anger and depression. "Why didn't Karl tell us he was getting references?" I asked Larry. "He didn't even give us an application form. It seems so deceptive, so unfair."

"I know. Karl probably asked us too soon. He should have waited to see if a couple he felt was more qualified showed up."

"And S.H. and Emily were our friends! He got to be base leader and later national director because you trusted and delegated."

"Well, there are misunderstandings in life, big bumps along the way. If we hang on and are faithful the Lord will lead us forward into missions, make us effective."

We kept praying and eventually felt peace to decline joining Karl's staff. We refined our five year goals, which included working until we paid off a home. Until then we would travel out to teach overseas once a year.

When the sky is dark with glowering clouds, sometimes brilliant streaks of light break through, glorifying the landscape. Our children's growth and development were that to us. Despite pruning and pain in one area, wholeness and fresh life appeared in another. In May Nick graduated from Oral Roberts University with a major in business, a minor in theology. Our family, my parents, and Nick's other dad cheered as he received his diploma.

He moved home that summer, developed his own window washing business, and later flew Stacey Matulla from Minnesota to visit us. She was lively and vibrant and seemed to complement Nick well. One evening he drove her to the Broadmoor Hotel for dinner…took her on a carriage ride…and later knelt and proposed by our dining room table.

When we arrived home later that night she was laughing and crying. "I had no idea Nick was going to propose tonight!" she said. "I'm so happy…what a perfect evening." She showed us the sparkling diamond on her left hand.

Some months later I drove home from Colorado Springs and up our driveway after a light rain. Clouds were scudding across the sky and the air was misty. I saw a large rainbow arching through the air just above our land, so I stopped the car halfway to the house and got out. Our rolling meadows were glistening green gold in the sunlight, with wind rippling the tall grasses. Far away on Ramah Road the school bus stopped and Jared jumped out at the corner. Seeing me in the distance, he walked fast then began running up the meadows, his backpack bouncing on his shoulder.

"Don't hurry," I yelled to him. "Take your time…see the rainbow!"

The wind tossed the words through the air, and he couldn't hear me. So I waited, loving the moment, loving my son running through the wind and mist and rainbow over our land. He arrived and I hugged him. "Isn't this beautiful!"

"Yeah," he answered. "And it's a long way to run home!" We laughed.

RECREATED IN THE CALL

MARATHON MENTALITY

For months that stretched into years I kept trying to refocus, to reshape my outlook into marathon endurance. We were headed to the mission field, but we were like Paul who had to make tents for awhile. And while we were back in the States we were launching our sons into life, into their callings.

We faithfully attended New Life as a family, had devotions, memorized scripture. We led the Saturday night prayer group at the church, with Jared playing worship music. Both sons attended youth or the college group, and Jared sang in the adult choir. As the church launched small groups we led some and eventually became section leaders over five to six groups, then zone leaders over 20-40 groups. We were committed and busy.

Nick was accepted as a youth pastor in North Carolina and later married Stacey at her parents' church in Hastings, Minnesota. They addressed each other after the vows, and Stacey said, "Thank you for keeping me pure, for being an example to me before the Lord…"

I was tearful, and the photographer later asked me, wiping her eyes, "They're really religious, aren't they?"

Each year we took a missions teaching trip, sometimes to two countries. S.H. and Emily welcomed us in Penang, and later Dass and Rani at their base south in Ipoh. Nepal, Ethiopia, and India also opened up, for DTS teaching or in the School of Biblical Studies. We began to support some of these leaders a small amount each month. We were planted in the States, but we were preparing for missions, doing whatever we could.

When we were elected elders at New Life (there were 35 couples—70 elders in what became a 14,000 member church) we began to lead a Sunday night elder prayer meeting. Our numbers were small, but through prayer we grew close in spirit.

Each year we came closer to getting a home paid for. Larry built houses by taking construction loans, and I nursed, doing 12 hour shifts working nights from 7pm to 7:30am. I drove home with blurry eyes, slapping my legs to stay awake. I loved the tiny babies in the NICU, the quiet late night hours, the extra pay for working the second shift. But at around 4am as I drank coffee to stay awake I would wonder to the Lord, "Is this the best way you can use me now? I don't feel like you called me to work here in the States. When will we break through into the big picture of missions, Lord?"

After helping Tony our neighbor with his cows Larry and I decided we didn't want to raise cattle to pay for missions. We were driving thirty miles to the Springs, sometimes twice a day. We divided the land and sold pieces of it, including our home on forty of the 160 acres. Then we rebuilt a slightly larger log home closer to town on Sweet Road that had less of a mortgage on it. That home had great views and a steep driveway which was challenging in winter.

Since Nick was now married, Jared was like an only child during his junior and senior years in high school. He was tall and dark haired, quiet, with a lively sense of humor. He practiced his classical and worship music late at night on our worn piano, singing resonantly. Darlene Baldwin his music teacher encouraged him to write songs. He wrote fun songs, worship songs, and some that were so deep and obscure I had to ask what they meant.

Over dinner we discussed life—church life, movies, girls, politics, callings. Jared was open with Larry and me, and we had sincere prayer in family devotions.

So when we found out Jared had been deceiving us in watching R rated movies at a friend's house, I was deeply hurt. We were in the living room, and I was kneeling on the floor. "How could you do this? You know the rules, and we've trusted you." I wiped my eyes.

"We want what's best for you, Jared," Larry said leaning forward, elbows on his knees. "Mom and I don't make any rules for you that we don't keep ourselves. They're guidelines to 'help our eyes be single, so our whole bodies will be full of light.' How can God use us if we take in garbage willingly?"

"I know," Jared said. He cleared his throat. "I'm sorry I deceived you. I won't do it again."

"I'm going to have to limit you from seeing those friends of yours, except at church for awhile," Larry told him.

"That's OK. I understand."

And we prayed together.

Jared graduated from Rampart High School in 1997 with a large party at our home on the hill. That summer we took him on a special graduation trip to Rome. We ate at the Piazza Navona where artists sold paintings, toured the Vatican…we even spent one night in Narni, the hilltop town northeast of Rome where I had stayed years before. We saw on a sign that Narni was the geographic center of Italy. I was amazed. Here we were, in the middle of Italy, and I felt like we were in the center of God's will for us at that time! Life was complete.

ARRESTED IN TURKEY

New Life Church was rocking. Our Wednesday night prayer meetings led by Pastor Ted were attracting hundreds of people. He usually taught 20 minutes on how to focus and pray in unity on one subject for five minutes intervals. Then as the band played worship music in the background, he challenged us to move as we prayed. "Whether walking, or sitting and rocking back and forth, five minutes of unified prayer with 500 people participating adds up to 2,500 minutes of prayer. That's over 41 hours of intercession rising to God's throne. Intensity and agreement do matter! The bowls of prayer should be filled, then they can be poured out upon the earth in answer to our prayers." (Rev.8:3-5)

Often we had 1,000 believers walking--or sitting and rocking--in the auditorium. There was a roar of intercession above the worship music. When the Gulf War began, a bulletin board was set up where people could post their loved ones names. Many would put their hands on the cards, praying fervently. We were amazed and grateful when victory came. God was answering our prayers!

Marti Anderson

In 1995 Pastor Ted also organized prayer journeys in conjunction with Louis Bush's 2000AD Prayer Movement. The goal was to send a team to every nation, to pray on site for every people group in that country to be reached with the Gospel. Larry, Jared and I joined Beverly Peguese, Jim and Judy Orred and others on a prayer journey to Turkey. Landing in Istanbul we saw the sights for a couple of days—the Topkapi Palace, and the 3,000-year-old Grand Bazaar. Then, crossing the Straits of Marmara by ferry we travelled to the seven church sites mentioned in Revelation chapters two and three, praying at each site.

After we all returned home Larry and I kept praying for Turkey. There were 64 million Islamic Turks in spiritual darkness, and according to statistics less than 1,000 Christians in the country. Friendly, hospitable people who needed truth. On that trip we had not passed out any scriptures and hardly witnessed to anyone. "Lord, would you want us to return next year and pass out Gospels, just the two of us?" Larry prayed.

After inquiry we found out we could purchase Turkish New Testaments in Istanbul. So for the next four years Larry and I returned...we were friendly tourists who drove in ever larger circles throughout western Turkey. We shopped, giving Injils (New Testaments) as gifts after we bought souvenirs or ate a snack. Driving through the countryside we stopped and took pictures of shepherds and farmers, giving them our Injil thank you gifts. Most were friendly and curious. And we prayed over those New Testaments. "Lord, help each person, each family to read these books. May your Word illumine their hearts."

One year Susan Finney our friend went with us, and for a few hours we lost her in Bergama (Pergamum). We had split up to shop—but she never showed up at our meeting place. We prayed earnestly in the car, driving throughout the town.

We finally saw her standing alone on a different street. "I must have left that one shop through the wrong door," she laughed. "I got lost after that."

"I'm so glad we found you!" I grinned. "I imagined you being married off to a carpet merchant...we would have had to tell your family you

222

were on a caravan expedition, and they might not have accepted it." We laughed.

On our fourth trip to Turkey we met up with Pastor Ted and Ross Parsley (our worship leader) in Izmir (Smyrna) where they were arranging the large 2,000AD gathering at the ruins of Ephesus. Thousands of Christians were to gather from all over the world in the amphitheater where "great is Diana of the Ephesians" had been shouted for two hours, in opposition to Paul's teachings.

We four ate dinner that night in downtown Izmir, and later in the evening the city celebrated joyously with cars honking in the streets because Turkey had won the World Cup over Germany.

The next summer we took a team to that large prayer gathering in Ephesus. The magnificent ruins were brilliant in the hot sunshine as we gathered in the huge amphitheater. Thousands of Christians from all over the world were seated on the ancient stone risers, many holding up their country's banners.

There was worship, then a choir from South Korea sang Handel's Hallelujah Chorus, accompanied by their orchestra. Peter Wagner spoke, as did Louis Bush, and Pastor Ted...culminating in a roar of spiritual warfare and prayer. At the end of four hours a generous offering was taken for Turkey's earthquake victims. We left sunburnt and filled with joy.

Our team travelled on to Bergama the next day to pass out Injils. That night I was getting ready for bed when police came, informing us we were all under arrest. The officers were brisk and pleasant in leading us to the police station. Some Muslim had been offended and complained, so they were investigating. After examining our passports and faxing headquarters they were suddenly friendlier. We had explained that we were part of the large Ephesus gathering...perhaps they were informed of that group giving $10,000 toward earthquake victims.

In any case, they shook hands with us saying "Thank you, thank you." The police chief smiled. "You are free to go now. Have a good journey."

The next day we headed to Denizli, a larger city further southeast. We still had more than two boxes of New Testaments to distribute, plus those in our backpacks. We had been told that Turkey had freedom of religion, so in a trial we could not be sentenced to prison. And since these Injils were printed in Turkey they were not illegal. Besides that, Turkey wanted to join the EU—surely they wouldn't want any bad press.

We checked into a large hotel and the next day after prayer split up into small groups. We were still friendly tourists shopping for souvenirs. All went well for several hours until a plain clothes policeman asked Larry and me to get into his car. Someone had complained that they had been religiously offended. A couple of our team saw us, and we waved to them. The policeman searched our van, taking the two boxes of New Testaments. We then handed the van keys to Bernie and Hannele our team members before the police drove us away.

In Denizli the police station was much larger, five stories high. We rode the elevator to the fourth floor where more officers gathered around us, more paperwork was generated…and no one spoke English well. We knew only a few words in Turkish, so until an interpreter could be found, we waited and silently prayed. I watched as an officer at one desk interestedly read one of our little red books.

When a teacher of English was found from the local high school, we were questioned thoroughly. Finally one officer asked, "Who paid for these books you are giving out?"

"My mother," I answered. "She wanted the people of Turkey to also know of the stories of Jesus in the Injil."

He looked surprised.

"We hear you have freedom of religion here," I continued. "In America we do also, and you could stand on a street corner and pass out the Koran in English. No one would stop you."

After some hours it was decided that we could be released. We were told to appear before a judge in the morning and pay a fine. They said we could go but they would keep our passports for the night.

Something broke in me. "I will not leave my passport. I will stay here for the night. I am not going."

"Marti," Larry interrupted. "It's going to be OK."

"No, I'd rather stay here."

After more discussion in Turkish they agreed to give me back my passport—they would just keep Larry's. We watched as our cardboard boxes of Bibles were tied up with brown twine and the knots sealed with red wax. I was fascinated…it looked rather medieval.

As we were leaving someone from the newspaper wanted to interview us, and bring an Islamic scholar in. "He can ask you questions about Christianity," the reporter said.

"Sure," Larry answered.

We were taken to a room where our friendly interpreter also waited. As the Islamic scholar questioned us I was amazed how the Holy Spirit gave us answers. This must have been how the disciples felt when they were brought before authorities, I thought.

Someone brought up President Clinton and referred to his recent affair with Monica Lewinsky. Larry began to weep. "We are ashamed of how he has been acting in his presidential office," Larry responded. "God wants us to live holy lives. We should obey Him, and leaders should especially be an example. I apologize for President Clinton."

All in the room were quiet, slightly embarrassed, and the meeting closed. As we walked out the interpreter invited us to his comfortable flat and served us tea. His young wife and child were polite and friendly.

We were dropped off at the hotel, and the team welcomed us joyfully. "We were so worried about you!" Hannele said, hugging me.

"We were going to fast and pray until you were released," Mike Harwood laughed, "but you've come just in time for dinner."

We feasted in the large dining room with other tourists and related the strange adventure. "We were wondering what the jails in Turkey would be like," Bernie laughed. "They might not supply toothbrushes."

The next morning we sat before a sober judge, who eyed us solemnly and demanded of me, "Uncross your legs!" Surprised, I quickly obeyed. It must be a mark of disrespect to sit that way, I decided.

We paid the $70 fine and drove north with the team, grateful and praying for direction. We had about 15 New Testaments left in our bags and distributed them carefully in the remaining days. Staying in Iznik on the east side of a lake one night, we viewed the ruins of Nicea, the site of a historic church council in 325AD. Asia Minor (now Turkey) had been scattered with churches then.

Some 700 years later the Oghuz Turks displaced them, eventually building mosques. Even the vast St. Sophia Church in Istanbul was turned into an Islamic place of worship. As we drove on winding roads we mused on the battle between light and darkness through the centuries. We were a small band of Christians sowing seeds of truth in the year 2,000.

"Lord, let these seeds grow into a large harvest of believers," we prayed.

A STUDENT AGAIN

Jared began attending Oral Roberts University in the fall of 1997, and it seemed strange to not have him home. We were slowly lowering our mortgage, clearing debt. And now we had college payments again— almost like another house payment—though Jared had some good scholarships.

One day Pastor Ted inquired, "When are you guys going to go back with Ywam into missions?"

"Probably in a couple of years," I answered wistfully.

"I think I've heard that from you before," he laughed.

"Well, we don't have any church that will support us fully, so we're trying to get a home paid for so we can rent it out."

"Oh." He nodded and turned to leave.

"And sometimes we sell our home and build another one to quicken the process. I get to decorate a new home, and we clear more debt."

"Good."

During the long hours of night nursing I felt like I was treading water in my missions calling—maintaining but making no progress. We were involved in small group ministry, but it didn't seem enough. Larry empathized with me. "You like teaching...why don't you get your masters at a seminary?"

So I began attending Fuller Seminary's extension in Colorado Springs, one class a semester, and fresh hope broke in. Theology, missions, leadership, Greek--these classes opened up worlds of understanding, knowledge, and relationships. I could reason, question, interact with peers and professors, and there was good purpose to it. I was preparing for teaching overseas!

Nick and Stacey had moved to Tulsa to staff a church, so Jared had family in Tulsa. And soon Madeline was born to Nick and Stacey in February of 1998—a tiny independent brown haired bundle of life. How could this small creature be our granddaughter? It seemed not long since Nick was small and strong and squalling!

The years melted together with work and studies. I began to take two classes at a time at Fuller. Jared graduated from ORU with a major in music composition in May of 2001. He was writing worship music and crossover songs—one that began, "Neptune's taming of the seahorse was rather late for an average year." He moved home and became a music intern at New Life. He loved writing music and became part of Desperation Band. Eventually he led worship at Saturday night and some Sunday morning services.

I also graduated in May, 2001 from Fuller Seminary, with Will Stoller-Lee the administrator commending each of our class magnanimously. I was even sad to be done with classes--learning had been so enjoyable.

"What if I go on and get a doctorate, Larry? A Doctor of Ministry. It's not as much work in original research as a PhD, like my dad had. So it would take possibly only two to three years."

"Check into it," Larry suggested.

I found out I would need seven courses to level into the program at Fuller Seminary in Pasadena, California, and I would have to live there for a time. At ORU in Tulsa it would only take three courses. If I took one intensive week-long course a month, doing pre and post course homework, I could complete the requirements during the fall of 2001, then enter their Doctor of Ministry program late, in February of 2002. I would then attend classes at ORU for two weeks every four months--for a total of two years--then work on my research project after that.

I was excited. I applied and was accepted.

The Friday before I left for my first class in Tulsa I attended noon prayer at the World Prayer Center, near New Life Church. Arriving early

I walked around the large building praying, where flags of the nations waved on tall flag poles. Today things seemed different somehow. I often saw angels in the Spirit as I interceded, but today there were many of them. They were surrounding the huge building clustered perhaps three deep. How strange!

At noon Ross Parsley led worship inside the building, and numbers of people walked around the room praying. Pastor Ted came in at the end, so I asked him what was happening at the church that day. I told him about the large numbers of angels.

"Well, there's a meeting of leaders here today," he answered.

"I don't think there's so many for that reason," I answered. "It must be for something else."

After driving ten long hours to Tulsa and staying in a hotel, I was eager to begin my fall classes. The first one was Old Testament Survey, and a lady professor engaged us all as she taught. It was the morning of Sept.11, 2001.

When we were interrupted by the news of the World Trade Center being bombed by a plane, there was shock and discussion. After the second plane ran into tower number two we were all called to chapel, and after prayer were dismissed for the day.

I sat in the hotel room watching the horrifying pictures on TV and talked to Larry on the phone. "It's awful, Honey. Maybe that's why I saw all those angels around the World Prayer Center. They were prepared to be summoned for this emergency? I never saw it like that before."

After completing my three courses that fall, I entered the Doctor of Ministry program in February of 2002 on the 12th floor of ORU's medical building. Tall, white haired Dr. Mayton was in charge, and he instructed the class of fifteen enthusiastically. "You want to track with the syllabus carefully to get the pre course homework done in plenty of time. We cover two courses each time you come, every four months." He smiled. "So it's best not to get behind—it'll be hard to catch up."

"When you write your post course papers you'll be laying groundwork for the applied research project you'll eventually choose and write in the third year. You each will narrow your focus to write an abstract—a long thesis statement—of what you want to research and prove in your area of ministry. Since each of you has had at least three years of active ministry, and you're from all over the world, it'll be interesting to hear your ideas."

I looked around. About half of our class was from Asia—India, Myanmar, and South Korea—and the rest from North America. There were four African Americans, three of them women. I was the only white woman.

The subjects were challenging--Leadership and Administration, Divine Healing, Pastoral Care and Counseling, Doctrine of God, Biblical Authority, Ministerial Identity, Preaching and Teaching. Larry was making good money building houses, and could cover the tuition. Some students had to work fulltime and had difficulty keeping up.

I usually studied at a particular Starbucks coffee shop in Colorado Springs. Sometimes Jared met me and we would catch up on life. He had recently bought a small house closer to downtown, and he and Larry had renovated it.

One morning we sat outside in view of Pikes Peak, sipping coffee. "I'm getting to know this one girl from New Life, Mom. She's tall, blond, beautiful. Has a good outlook on life. Is mature, loves the Lord."

"Wow. Has she been to college?"

"Yeah. She's a grade school teacher—is also working on her masters in counseling. And she drives a classy car."

"Well, that's important." We laughed.

"She's from Wisconsin. Grew up in a nice Catholic family. She's coming over with others to decorate my house for the young adults Christmas party. You can show up to help, and meet her."

I did arrive to decorate, and was introduced to Megan. She was friendly and engaging, seemed to have a gift for leadership and drawing out the best in people. As she and I wrapped Jared's circular metal stairs with Christmas greenery I wondered, "Will this girl be my future daughter-in-law?" She certainly was pretty.

We invited Megan to join Jared when we had him for dinner once a week. Discussion was lively…and I noticed in between courses Jared would often hold Megan's hand, kissing it. I was impressed. "Larry, I don't remember you doing that while we were dating," I said laughing.

"No, I didn't," he smiled. "But I had other good qualities."

"Well, you kissed well!"

In a few months Jared shared his plan with us. He had been to Wisconsin and asked Megan's dad for her hand in marriage. And he had our blessing. "I want you guys to be a part of the engagement surprise," he said. "Dad, my friend Joe is going to pick Megan up at her classroom, with roses from me. I'll get permission from her principal for a sub to take over for her that day. I want you to fly her to Montrose, where Mom and I will meet you at the airport. Mom, you and I will get there the night before, and I'll fix sandwiches in the motel room. Then I'll take Megan to Ouray for a picnic and propose...you know how beautiful the mountains are in Ouray. You and Dad can fly home, and we'll arrive home later that evening. How about it?"

"Wow. That's an incredible proposal you're planning, Jared. Do you think she can live through the surprise?"

"Well, I don't want her ever to forget it," he chuckled.

Larry renewed his flying license, and all happened as planned. But the day was so windy, the plane bounced high as Larry and Megan landed in Montrose. We hugged, then waved Jared and Megan goodbye as they drove off to their picnic. Later we flew home in the Cessna, picking our way through scattered clouds. When we landed east of Colorado Springs, it was just before a blustery rainstorm. Larry handed the Cessna over to the rental agency and we thanked God for protection.

As Jared and Megan made wedding plans I continued attending ORU every four months. A friend of Jared's, Dr. Leanne Polvado opened her beautiful home to me in Tulsa—a great blessing.

Each week of class was unique, with a different instructor introducing truths we students could grapple with. Discussion was encouraged, so I often asked questions or made comments and tried to be concise. Other students also made comments, but the Asians—half the class—rarely spoke. Stanley, an older student, seemed to dominate the discussion time, often meandering off subject. After some minutes he would return to the main point, and the instructor would patiently respond.

One week the professor was covering systems in church government and congregational life, telling us that problems or glitches in systems generally work themselves out. I was intrigued. The professor and I were in the elevator after lunch one day, so I inquired of him, "What if a student is long winded and slows the class down. Would you correct him, in the system of a classroom?"

"No," he answered, smiling. "In the classroom context this problem would just work itself out."

Was that my answer? Later in the day as Stanley began monologuing I decided to help the system. I raised my hand and the professor acknowledged me. "I know we all have equal time to share, so when I have a long question or comment I try to talk fast. Lately I've been very restless and impatient because you Stanley make many comments and often wander off the subject. Since we only have so much time to hear the teaching, could you keep to the point?"

An awkward silence followed. I could tell the Asians were aghast. According to their cultures I had been very rude. Stanley then defended himself. "I think I keep to the subject with my stories and comments, and I'm just expressing myself."

There was more discussion and the professor quietly listened. Then one of the black women spoke. "No, Stan, you do take up a lot of time. You start a subject, talk in a circle, and finally come back to the point."

"Well, if you say so I guess I don't have to talk. I can be quiet."

Class resumed with neither Stanley nor me saying much that day or the next. We heard more from the professor...and the Koreans, Indians and Burmese slowly began to comment more often.

In August Megan walked down the aisle of the World Prayer Center with her father. As she slowly proceeded, each of her fourth grade students stood in the aisle and handed her wild flowers, which made up her bouquet. She was glowing, radiant, and Jared standing by Pastor Ted looked as if he had won the world.

I wept in quiet joy. In the midst of our struggles God had led us to a great church with an amazing youth group to help our sons. He gave us gracious daughter-in-laws, and was establishing our sons in life callings. And as He was paying off our home I was able to receive excellent training for future teaching. His plans were so good!

That fall Larry and I flew to Pune, India and I taught a week in a Ywam school for my research project, giving pretests and posttests. The project-- The Impact of Developing a Mission Statement Upon International Christian Leaders—was interesting to both Indian students and staff. We developed relationships with some of the leaders and began to support them a little each month. Prabha, Mary, Vijayan, and Neibano became long term friends.

In the spring of 2004 I defended my research project before an astute committee of four, which included Dr. Mayton. He shook my hand at the end. "Let me be the first to congratulate you, Dr. Anderson." I smiled and nearly hugged my dignified professor. Dr. Mayton's encouragement had helped propel me through the process.

I walked down the graduation aisle with classmate Harrison Haokip from Myanmar in May. We were the first two of our class to finish research projects and graduate. Mom and Dad were there to rejoice with us afterwards. Seasoned and worn from 38 years on the mission field, they were my heroes.

CAIRO MACCHIATO

In the fall of 2004 Larry and I rented out our log home in Black Forest and packed up to move to India. After twelve long years a home was paid for, and rent from the lower apartment would help support us. We requested $800 a month travel support from New Life, and were offered $1,000—so encouraging, since this would help us teach throughout Asia more freely.

Nick and Stacey now lived in Birmingham, Alabama involved in business and their church, with three children—Madeline, Hudson and Macy. Jared and Megan had little Everett, with another son on the way.

Jared saw us off at the Denver airport. After two days of flying east, Prabha met us in Mumbai with a van to accommodate our multiple bags.

"How are you, Brother Larry and Sister Marti? It's so good to see you." This Indian Ywam leader was small and strong, and radiated joy through brown chiseled features.

"Prabha, I can't believe we're here! How is Mary doing, and how is the Bible school?"

"Good," he answered. "We are in our new location in the hills at Lonavala. Mary and I live in a room at the big base."

We drove through miles of slums and then high rises on our way east from Mumbai. While climbing the hills toward Lonavala four hours later we were still in misty smog. The Youth with a Mission base was on the edge of town, white two storied buildings climbing the hill among spreading trees and tropical greenery. Mary greeted us shyly, her dark hair framing a beautiful smile. And our joyful friend Nibano welcomed us too. An articulate writer, her emails had kept us informed of Indian mission life.

Since there was an area leaders gathering at the base, we would be housed in a hotel in town. During the next week our joy at arriving was tempered with jetlag, heat, and the claustrophobic hotel room. Friends helped us shop for a car in Pune, further east. Our two hour train rides to and from there took us past crowded towns, golden fields plowed by oxen, and beggars forlorn at train stations. Riding with us were women dressed in brilliant saris, clean schoolchildren bearing backpacks, business men perusing newspapers, and laborers worn and dozing from work. An astonishing microcosm of Indian life was in one railway car.

We met petite, energetic Anna who was attending the Ywam leaders meeting in Lonavala. She was a Brazilian leader from the smaller base in Goa, an hour's flight south. We had been emailing her about the possibility of living in Vasco Da Gama, a town in Goa near the Indian Ocean. She welcomed us warmly...and after a few days it was decided we would be based there and fly in and out to teach.

Larry was still trying to get an international driver's license, so when we finally bought the white Maruti car an Indian friend had to drive us the bumpy winding kilometers to Vasco da Gama.

I envisioned Vasco as a large white washed town with European flavor. I knew that many English vacationed there. Portugal had originally colonized this province, and Catholics had built stately white churches. We were disappointed to find the town was old and dreary, with cows roaming the streets, walls moldy from past monsoons, and electric wires hung helter skelter from shops to market. Only the beachside hotels were elegant.

Anna and Gloria welcomed warmly into their comfortable apartment. We had dinner, and they offered us a bedroom until we could locate housing. "What kind of ministry do you have, Gloria?" I inquired as we ate. She was taller, with thick brown hair, and dark expressive eyes.

"I teach children from the slums," she answered. "I love kids, so I help as many as I can in the small room we've rented at the village. As they learn the alphabet we also teach Christian principles and hygiene. It's rewarding...the children and their parents are so grateful."

"And you guys are supported by your churches back home?"

"And by family."

"What a blessing. You're laying up treasure in Heaven!"

"We all are...and I have the children's love," she said, laughing.

In the coming days we met more Indian and Brazilian staff at the base, which was located in a large home in a sprawling subdivision. Gloria inquired of neighbors for an empty flat and located a second floor apartment with metal stairs to a bedroom. After negotiations we agreed on rent, signed a lease, and drove winding roads to the larger town of Panaji (Panjim) to buy furniture, cookware, and bedding. After years of living in cool Colorado the Indian heat baked energy out of us. We found that the coolest spot was in our air conditioned car...that as we drove life became bearable.

Staff meetings and prayer twice a week, study for teaching, walks on the beach in the evenings. We began to preach at a local church once a month, then taught the DTS students when school started at the base. We flew in and out of the small airport to Mumbai when we had other speaking engagements, but had little day to day ministry in Goa.

One week we taught in Addis Ababa, Ethiopia at the invitation of Dass and Rani, our Malaysian friends from Penang. They had been students in 1992, and were now leading the work in Ethiopia. Our third time teaching in Addis, this week's subject was on the five stages of growth in leadership, and the class was eager, receptive.

We were home a few days when I shared with Larry, "You know, I fight depression every time we come back to such a quiet place. Do you think we made a mistake in moving to Vasco? We spend so much money flying in and out of Mumbai. We've taught locally some, but we could be busier in a big hub."

"So what are you suggesting?"

"Well, Cairo is central to Africa, Europe, and Asia, and they have Ywam work there."

"Let's call Dass in Addis. He knows leaders in Cairo. Maybe he can recommend someone."

When we telephoned, Dass was enthusiastic. "Yes, I know a good leader in Cairo named Moses, in charge of urban ministries. He's Korean—you could perhaps join his team. I'll call him."

After Christmas back in the States we stopped to visited Moses and Joanne in their Cairo apartment. "We would love for you to join our team," Moses said, leaning forward on the couch. "We are mostly Korean, but you could fit right in. You would be the grandparents...you know we honor those older than us," he said smiling.

"I see you have maps all over your living room walls," I said.

"Yes, Moses loves maps," Joanne said, offering us more cookies.

"It helps you to envision the mission fields of the world," he responded. "Then you can pray. If God leads you here there are two Bible schools you could teach in. Victory Bible Institute needs instructors, and another one north of us. And I know of a couple who are moving back to England—you could perhaps rent their place."

"That would be wonderful."

"Probably you could buy dishes, bedding, many household items," Joanne added. "We can introduce you to them tomorrow."

Before we left for India we talked to the leaders of both Bible schools and had the third floor apartment lined up. We would buy their household items for a reasonable sum...and many flowering plants would be left on the balconies. I was amazed and grateful.

On our taxi drive north through Cairo to the airport we passed through miles of sand colored apartment buildings. The pyramids were far to the south, on the edge of the vast city. The traffic was thick, and the air heavy with smog. Such a condensation of people in one place! When the mosque prayer call rang out, the whole city reverberated. I was struck with the enormity of Cairo—20 million Egyptians—most of whom did not know Jesus.

As we flew back to Goa via Mumbai, I thought of the masses in both metropolises The world was so big! How could the Gospel reach every city, every people group? We needed to multiply ourselves in discipling others through these schools.

"Please, Lord, make us effective," I prayed, looking out the plane's window.

In the spring months we taught books of the Bible for Prabha in the School of Biblical Studies at the Lonavala base. That school was smaller, the students more intense as they did hours of inductive Bible study. I gave context and historical background, and at the end Larry and I prayed for them together.

One evening Mary served chapattis, delicious dahl and rice as little Jerusha toddled around us. "We want to multiply these schools, and also work with the poor in the slums," Prabha shared. "There is need for teams to multiply this work."

"We pray for you guys daily. And we want to keep helping support you. You also, Nibu," I said, nodding to her. We would teach in her DTS.

In a few months we packed up and had a farewell dinner with Anna, Gloria, and the team. They were like family...we would miss them. But in Cairo we would be more centrally located.

The most stressful part of moving to Egypt was not settling into our third floor apartment or working with the Korean team. It was the challenge of retrieving our excess luggage—air cargo that arrived a few weeks later. Day after day as Larry checked with the cargo company in Mumbai, the clerk was in turns emphatic, vague, or conciliatory. "If you're not sure where the luggage is and when it will come, perhaps I need to fly to Mumbai and find the luggage myself!" Larry told him, exasperated.

But at last it arrived...and we spent one whole day in customs, walking our papers through various offices for stamps of approval. Near the end of the line someone discovered that we had a printer in the luggage.

"Oh, you will have to go to a building in Tahrir Square to retrieve that, in downtown Cairo. You need a special stamped paper to import a machine like that."

"I can't believe it," I muttered to Larry.

"Why did you tell him we had one?" Larry asked me later.

"He asked if we had anything electronic in the luggage. I was trying to be honest."

"Well, maybe here they're concerned with people copying propaganda and distributing it."

Another day we found the downtown office, and a genial official signed a permit to retrieve our printer.

In the following weeks Larry painted our apartment a cheerful light yellow and we hung red curtains from India, pictures, and woven tapestries. We befriended neighbors and had the Korean team over for prayer and pastries. We attended the bimonthly city team meeting and got better acquainted with the main Ywam leader and various ministries in the city. And every Friday morning we attended Maadi Community Church.

Since Muslims were off work on Fridays, the Christians gathered for worship that day. Our pavilion church with open sides resounded with worship and good preaching from Pastor Petrescue, as uniformed soldiers stood guard round the church compound. In fact, every block in Maadi was guarded by two policemen, to protect the foreigners from terrorism.

I grew accustomed to them as we walked the mile down Road Nine to Grecos, our favorite coffee shop. I felt safer, but I also felt sorry for their long hours of boredom in the extreme summer heat or winter cold. As we began teaching two or three times a week we trudged the long mile to Grecos almost every day. It was a great place to study.

On the way, we passed small Arabic tea shops where men sipped chai and smoked water pipes, then the train station where business men hustled past and thickly clad women trod heavily, carrying bags of vegetables from the market. Another block or two and the stores became more elegant. Tourists browsed in handicraft shops, a guard stood by a bank. A little further, after passing under tall trees and a beggar or two, there was Grecos Coffee Shop. Amir or Walid would set steaming lattes before us topped with heart shaped froth, after we walked in with our backpack of books.

I loved the study of the Bible and life principles, I loved teaching them. Had we found our niche of ministry? Was I at last finding my tribe?

CLIMBING MOUNTAINS

The students at Victory Bible Institute were mostly Sudanese immigrants who were eking out a living in a foreign land. Having Christian background, they were hungry to learn more of God's word, and the large room was packed with around 100 students. But the room's one small air conditioner could not lower the temperature much. Once I had to walk out for fresh air, the smell of sweat was so strong. They listened intently, took notes, asked questions.

Festus the school leader from Nigeria interpreted for us into Arabic, and exercised good discipline. One young man didn't know Arabic well, so needed extra interpretation from a friend into his tribal language. All this translation took time, so we chose our words well and made concepts simple.

I was reminded of the large Sunday gatherings in the Ilaga Valley when my dad's sermons had to be relayed to the crowds into two languages. We were carrying on the Lord's work, in our time and generation. It was so fulfilling—we walked home tired and joyful.

Another semester we taught the second year students on marriage and family in an upstairs room that was cooler. The class was smaller, around 50, and seemed more mature, with both Egyptians and Sudanese. One time I finished sharing on the woman's role in marriage during the first half of class, and then it was Larry's turn. After giving scriptures Larry began to apply them.

"Jesus is the Head of the church, right? He is the one we worship and obey. But in truth He is always serving us. We are his bride, and He nourishes and cares for us."

"So, men, what is our role as the head of the family? When we come home after work—do we expect to be served, to be waited on? Should we also desire to serve, to meet our wives and children's needs?"

I watched the class from where I sat. The women looked alert and smiling, the men serious and a little uncomfortable.

Later during break an older man took Larry aside. "I think this truth you are teaching about serving may work for the younger men," he said. "But it may not work for the older men. We are very set in our ways."

"I understand," Larry answered thoughtfully. "But God's Word, his instructions are for every time and culture. He must give us all grace to obey."

"Yes, but I believe it is more difficult for Egyptian men."

When we later taught at the four year Bible college we rode the train north at dusk. The metro was not as crowded as in India, but just as exotic. Beautiful girls in jeans boarded wearing layers of bright colored head scarves, sweater tops, and well applied makeup. A young man might carry her backpack, but there was never public display of affection. More mature women wore thick black galabias in the heat...many were overweight, and they looked tired, with parcels and children. Men read papers... some recited the Koran softly, especially during Ramadan. Always there was order, politeness.

The students at this Bible College were mostly Egyptian, better educated, and asked good questions. Dr. Laban interpreted for us, an expansive man both in size and length of words. Late at night as we rode the metro home, I would muse on our unique privilege of sowing seeds of truth in this ancient city.

Needing more efficient transportation Larry and I finally shopped to buy a motorcycle, and settled on a 400cc Honda. It was black, shiny, and fast. I prayed sincerely for protection as Larry swerved in heavy traffic at busy roundabouts.

We began attending Maadi Community Church's cell groups. In the vast Islamic atmosphere each small group was an oasis of light and life in the middle of a work week. I met Eileen from England who became a dear friend. She took Larry and me shopping to Khan el-Khalili, Cairo's great bazaar and led us to unusual shops of antiques, jewelry, and glassware. And we developed other friends, like Mike and Marlene from the States with whom we began to eat out every Thursday night. One favorite place was TGI Friday's, next to the Nile. Eating hamburger and fries we could watch the sailboats and dinghy's drift by, slanting rays of sunshine glittering across the gray-blue water.

As we continued to study late mornings at Grecos Café I was unaware of how encultured we were becoming. One day some tourists walked in, one of them in a blouse with thin spaghetti straps.

"Look at that woman, Larry. I can't believe how bare she's dressed."

"Yeah," Larry agreed. "Here in Cairo she looks like a prostitute."

"I suppose we're thinking like Egyptians now," I laughed. "In the States she wouldn't even be noticed."

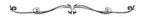

In between school terms we flew to Holland to teach young people at a DTS in Amsterdam and later to another one near Birmingham, England on "Discover Your Destiny," how to cooperate with God in finding His calling on your life. Later in Denmark we taught at a Family Ministries School on marriage and family life. In each setting we tried to relate according to the age group and culture.

Our leader Moses asked me to teach the books of Hebrews and James in his School of Biblical Studies at a base south of Cairo in the Egypt desert. Each book would take a week, or about 15 hours of instruction.

"I don't know, Moses. I haven't taught Hebrews in depth before. Are you sure you can't find someone more experienced?"

"I'm sure you can do it, Marti."

After working with the outlines and historical context I took the challenge. And the Lord did enable me to teach…I grew richer from the study. Each late afternoon Larry and I walked out of the compound into golden sun stretching across desert shrubs and grazing sheep.

"This is just like it was in the days when Israel lived in Egypt," Larry said.

"So peaceful. I love it," I answered. "Only they had to work hard to make bricks!"

Back in Cairo where the air was smoggy we began having bouts of upper respiratory infection. We made friends with a local pharmacist who prescribed whatever antibiotic he thought best. We didn't have to see a doctor first. But at various times we each were bedridden—good times to meditate, pray, watch pink bougainvillea on the balcony bob in the dusty breeze.

After we had been in Cairo about a year Moses invited the team to have a retreat in a resort at the Red Sea, asking Larry and me to teach on forming five-year goals. There were around 10 of us, a mix of Koreans, Americans and one Egyptian. The resort was luxurious, with bright stucco buildings near the glittering blue sea.

Each morning we sat in a circle. Larry and I taught how to form five year goals through a simple exercise. "Your goals need to be specific and measurable, Larry instructed them. And set within a time frame."

"After you define them well, you could even make a spread sheet," I added. "If God has encouraged you to believe for finishing college, writing a book, or learning a language within five years, you could make a list of what you would want to have accomplished at the end of each year. A deadline keeps you focused on finishing that particular goal. And each goal builds on the one before it."

The next day each team member shared their measurable goals, and we were amazed by one of the young Korean women. "How did you think this through so well, Sunshine?" I exclaimed. You taped together all these sheets of paper to detail your steps, month by month and year by year."

She laughed. "Well, I want to learn Arabic, develop my ministry to older people here, and eventually get a degree, so I thought writing each monthly step would be helpful."

"Sunshine has us all beat," Larry declared. "I've never been that specific, myself."

"This has been very helpful," Moses said, holding his list up. "Joanne and I are praying about next steps as our children graduate from high school. Goals change as we enter new stages of life."

Back in Cairo at Grecos we met Alice, one of the Korean team. "Your goal setting was so helpful to me," she said, sipping coffee. I'm setting new objectives and enlarging the ones I have as I teach children here."

"I'm so glad, Alice. I'm impressed with your commitment."

"My sister is coming to visit me from Korea. I want to show her some sights, and one of them is to take her up Mt. Sinai. Have you been there? You could come also."

"No…we actually haven't been out of Cairo much, except to Alexandria and the base. Would you like to go, Larry?"

"Sure," he said, looking up from his book. How do we get there, Alice?"

"Well, we could take Moses' van, since they'll be out of town. We would drive to Sharm-El- Sheikh, which will take all day, and sleep there. Then the next night we drive to St. Catherine's Monastery, and around midnight ride a camel up the mountainside. You trek the last few hours to reach the peak by sunrise. It's beautiful, but very tiring."

I took a deep breath. "That would be a real adventure. Riding up Mount Sinai on a camel."

"It is," Alice laughed. But I've done it so many times with outreach teams, I'm not excited anymore. However, my sister will love it."

A few weeks later we drove to Sharm-El-Sheikh and wandered around the modern white washed city sightseeing, then took a late afternoon nap at our hotel. That evening, with Alice and her sister in the van, we tried to find the road to St. Catherine's Monastery.

"Why don't they mark the roads better," I wondered, as we drove up yet another highway.

"There are few road signs," Alice agreed. "I suppose all the bus tour guides know the way already."

It was around midnight when we found the site. Tour buses and cars lined the parking lot. And all available camels had been hired out—not one was left. But Alice was undaunted. "We have flashlights. I can find the way."

We trudged up the mountain for around two hours when we began to meet guides leading camels downward, having left their tourist burdens near the top. Alice bartered with a guide who had four camels and got him to agree to rent each for $10. We mounted, and I gripped the saddle horn desperately as my white camel heaved upward. Hamid the guide led the way through the darkness.

Onward, upward, I swayed back and forth. My camel was perilously close to rock precipices on the left, so I tried leaning to the right. It made no difference—each camel had his own idea about safety. I hugged the camel tightly with my legs, and tried to calm myself.

"This is exciting, Larry! How are you girls doing?"

"We're fine," Alice answered. "I'm so glad we're on a camel and not walking."

After a couple of hours my legs went numb. I rearranged my scarf and shivered in the light jacket as we swayed, on and on. The black rocks around us began to glow gray green in early morning light. The landscape was surreal…this was like a movie…was I dreaming?

"Larry, this is amazing. Can you believe we're doing this?"

"Climbing Mt. Sinai on camels, in the early morning! It's unreal."

Brighter and brighter the morning dawned, until you could look left upon vistas of mountains and valleys. Finally we stopped on a broad ledge of rock and dismounted among scores of other camels. We ordered hot tea and candy bars from a Bedouin kiosk, took pictures, and rested.

"Alice, I've never had an adventure like this. Thank you for bringing us with your sister!"

"You're welcome, Marti." She smiled, her dark eyes crinkling with joy. "This is a big memory."

As we climbed two more hours on foot toward the last summit we met hundreds of tourists descending the mountain who had watched the sunrise from the peak. We stepped aside on the narrow path as each tour group passed us. Larry was recovering from the flu, so we also paused for him to rest. "We could stop here, view the mountains, and go back," I finally suggested.

"No, we've come this far. I want to make it to the top."

Finally we reached the summit, and sat near a small chapel. Gray blue mountain ranges tumbled below us, everywhere we looked. The world was so vast, so bare and majestic. God was great, the Creator of it all.

"God, you're so good to us," Larry said, looking around. "You brought us here, and we're able to view your wonders here in the land of Egypt. Thank you for your love, your mighty works. May the peoples of the earth come to know you, to love you."

"Amen," we agreed.

As we rested I mused on the years of preparation and pain, the many steps of obedience in my life to reach this summit. Living among the Dani tribe, Bible college, divorce. Working with single parents with Larry in Minneapolis, beginning a school in Penang. Years of nursing and building and cell group ministry in Colorado Springs. Living and teaching in India, and now Cairo. Each step had prepared us for the next vista or mountain range to be climbed in God's calling. Each stage, every step was important.

Moses had been prepared till he was 80 years old, Abraham until he was 100. Paul had years of training and desert experience until he was sent out from Antioch with Barnabas. Mountaintops were like milestones. At the summit you could remember the past journey, and look to future horizons. And remember that faithfulness matters. Faithfulness each step of the way.

We descended the mountain slowly, on shaky knees. The sun was scorching the earth now, and we were exhausted. But it had been worth it.

We collapsed into the van several hours later and dozed in air conditioning as Larry chugged back to Sharm El Sheikh. The next day we drove back into Cairo, quiet much of the way.

We were the same people, but changed. From being on the mountain.

THE FALL OF TWO PASTORS

Each summer we returned to the States, visiting with family and friends. And Larry did construction work to pay for the trip.

The summer of 2006 we especially enjoyed worshipping at New Life Church, and hearing Pastor Ted Haggard preach. He was a fine teacher.

The current sermon series was on how our spiritual life corresponded to the Old Testament tabernacle—the Outer Court, Inner Court, and Holy of Holies. We could linger in the Outer Court after salvation, or press into the Inner Court and receive the baptism in the Holy Spirit. As we lived a life of worship and obedience we could abide in the presence of God— the Holy of Holies.

Being the head of the National Association of Evangelicals, Pastor Ted travelled often. When he preached on Sunday he might have just returned from an overseas trip and be jetlagged. After awhile I noticed the first half of his sermons becoming repetitive—he summarized last Sunday's sermon in the first half, then began new material in the last half. After weeks of slowly moving through the tabernacle series, I wondered when we could hear more fresh material.

"Doesn't Pastor Ted realize he's repeating himself?" I asked Larry as we drove home one Sunday. "It seems like he preaches almost the same sermon. He's speaking to thousands of people--you'd think he'd prepare better."

"Maybe he forgets where he left off. Or maybe he's trying to let the same truth sink in deeper," Larry reflected.

We made an appointment to see Ted and discuss our future before we left for Cairo. He was vigorous and direct as usual, friendly…and mentioned that he was struggling with high blood pressure. "And they want to draw blood to do tests, but I don't want them to."

"Oh—we'll be praying for you," I said.

He was standing in his large office by the bookshelves, and looked hard at me as if he would say more. But he didn't. The moment passed and we said goodbye.

Weeks later, back in Cairo I called Sherrill my friend and asked about church. "What is Pastor Ted preaching on now?"

"Well, we're still on the tabernacle series," she answered.

"Amazing."

As we continued our teaching and travel in and out of Cairo, this fall there seemed to be more spiritual warfare. I struggled with anxiety for our safety, even though the soldiers stood guard on every block, and each church service was well guarded. Once, walking past a local Islamic school, young boys began throwing rocks as us.

The beloved Pastor Petrescue from Maadi Community Church unexpectedly died from a fall from his apartment building. He had forgotten his keys when he went up on the flat roof. Closing the door, he had no way of unlocking it to descend the stairs. He was letting himself down to an outside balcony by a cord when it broke, and he fell seven stories to his death. The church was in mourning...we were all affected.

As I studied to teach Romans, Larry began praying with another intercessor at church. Maadi needed much prayer in this season, as of course did all of Cairo. One day Larry looked up from his Bible reading. "You know, I enjoy praying with Mike, and I care about the students here. But I miss building projects. There's a part of me that's not being used. And we're sick so often. Sometimes I feel rather ineffective."

"That's true. It sure is a fight to stay healthy. What I miss most is being with the kids and grandkids. One of our five year goals is to have spiritual input into their lives. It's harder to do that from a distance."

"We talked to Pastor Ted last summer about moving back and travelling in and out from Colorado Springs," Larry mused. "If I were building part time we could support ourselves more."

One evening we received an email from the New Life elder group. There was to be a meeting of the elders...allegations had been made on a Denver radio station about Ted consorting with a male prostitute. It seemed unreal.

Another night before I checked emails I saw on the MSN front page the picture of a man that looked like Ted. "Look, Larry. A soldier must have died—and he looks just like Pastor Ted!"

Larry came to look, then we read the caption together. "It is Ted," Larry breathed. He's being investigated about those charges. The man who accuses him says he also took methamphetamines."

We watched BBC and CNN most nights...and now Pastor Ted was on the news. We watched as he denied wrong doing to reporters, looking so sincere. His wife Gayle who sat next to him in the car looked traumatized. Soon after we began to read stories about him in the Egyptian Gazette.

One day we telephoned Jared who was on staff at New Life. "How are you doing," Larry asked.

"Well, I'm just putting one foot in front of the other, every day. I hang out with other staff to make sense of what's happening. It's like a bad dream."

"I can imagine," Larry answered.

"The overseers have been called in, Pastor Ted's been asked to stay away from the church. Ross Parsley the music pastor has been asked to be interim pastor.

"So the allegations are really true?"

"The prostitute guy had a recording of Pastor Ted's voice on the telephone, and the voiceprint matches. The newspapers in Denver and Colorado are following this closely, and the news on TV.

"Unbelievable. Well, we're praying for you all."

"Thanks—we need it."

We finished our teaching assignments that fall and packed to move home. "This seems strange, Larry," I said, as I took down wall hangings and packed books. "We've been here a year and a half...I never thought we'd move home so quickly."

"Well, maybe it's like a wartime evacuation, Larry answered. "Our home church is in crisis. Perhaps the arm of the church can't support what the hand is doing in missions. Not just financially, but spiritually. I have a peace that we're moving home at the right time."

"Well, Moses and Joanne are moving back to Korea for a time, so their teenagers adapt to the culture there. The whole team is changing."

"I'm looking forward to spending more time with the grandkids. God will use this for all of our good."

Our plane left in the middle of the night. We had already said sad farewells to our barista friends at Grecos, and given dishes and blankets to young friends at church who were getting married. As we lugged our large suitcases down three flights of marble stairs late that night, the elderly landlady opened her door to wave goodbye.

We flew into Denver with snow and warm hugs from Jared and Everett, who was now one year old and toddling. Chubby Beckett was home with Megan, in their cozy home near downtown Colorado Springs. "He's playing Baby Jesus in New Life's nativity program," Megan told us, laughing. "He's been pretty busy." Our Christmas with them was sweet.

Later we celebrated with Nick and Stacey in Birmingham, Alabama. Madeline was now eight, articulate, and artistic. Hudson a blond six year old was quiet and thoughtful. Macy their two year old chortled with glee over her small camel from Cairo.

My parents were now retired in Lexington, Kentucky, attending an Alliance church that they had helped launch years ago. They loved hearing our stories, seeing our pictures of camel riding up Mt. Sinai.

Larry began construction work again and we picked up with the Sunday evening elder prayer at New Life. Occasionally there were larger elder meetings where overseers or Ross Parsley exhorted us to be steady in the church, as others would follow our example. A letter of apology from Pastor Ted was read one Sunday at the services. Later a pastoral search committee was formed. Ross Parsley had been an excellent worship pastor...now he was becoming a good preacher.

We were encouraged. We had the praying elder group over for a potluck meal. "It's kind of like Dad died, and big brother has taken over the family," I commented, as we ate. "If we get another pastor from outside, it will be like stepdad comes in. New Life may change into a whole different church.

"Yes, Ross is doing a good job." Molly said. "We're still like a big family."

"The search committee will only put up one candidate at a time for the church to vote on," another added. "This may be a long process, finding the right pastor."

Brady Boyd from Dallas came to candidate, and preached three times. He was younger than Ted, a solid clear teacher, but without the charisma that Pastor Ted had shown.

The church voted...and only Brady Boyd was on the ballot. If he was not voted in, I heard, the search committee would take more months—maybe a year—to offer another candidate.

"Why didn't they allow us to choose between Ross and Brady?" I wondered to Larry. "Many people would like Ross to stay."

"I don't know," Larry answered. "It would make more sense to give us a choice."

Brady Boyd became our new pastor. The elder group was dissolved...we could stay a part of the prayer team who ministered up front at the end of every service, but our close association was ended. Many did not understand. "Why were we all asked to stay steady, pray, and counsel encouragingly, but now we're disbanded?" one in our elder prayer group asked.

"I don't know," I answered. "It's amazing how much freedom God gives to a pastor in how to lead his church."

As the months passed church bylaws were changed by a committee and new staff hired. Jared stayed on at New Life and continued to lead worship sometimes. We were told there would be no more opportunity for the gifts of the Spirit to operate freely. Pastor Brady wanted only staff or visiting ministers to prophesy in a specified service, after some teaching on prophecy.

After being used for years in that gift—along with other members—I was mystified. "How can Pastor Brady change our church in the area of the spiritual gifts?" I wondered to Larry. "New Life is a charismatic, full gospel church."

"Well, he evidently wants the gifts to operate in smaller settings. He only wants staff or ministers to be used in the gifts in a large service. He tried to explain that when he and Pam came for dinner weeks ago."

"Well, we're ordained. Ted trusted us for years. You were used in giving words also."

"That's all changed now," Larry answered sadly.

The church support for our teaching travels continued through the spring until a newly hired missions pastor changed the support allotments. We taught in Kyrgystan and India, then began to just travel just once a year to India to teach in Bangalore and Lonavala, trusting the Lord for expenses.

FINDING MY TRIBE

The Lord had planted us in many locations, but this time we felt a special joy in living in Colorado Springs near family, helping Megan with the grandkids when Jared travelled with his band. To Everett and Beckett were added spunky Francie and amiable Lyla. Nick and Stacey eventually moved to Orlando, Florida, so it was harder to keep up with Maddie, Hudson, and Macy. We missed them. Each time we saw them they were taller, more mature.

Larry found fulfillment in building houses, and we led prayer groups in our home. I wanted to teach again and asked God to open doors for me. After instructing two elective classes for Kings Seminary at New Life Church I applied at Pikes Peak Community College (PPCC).

"I see you offer New Testament as a class. I have a lot of background in Bible history and theology...is there any way I might teach it?" I inquired of Richard Trussell, the chair of the department. He was middle aged, brown haired, with perceptive eyes. I found out he was formerly a Lutheran pastor.

"Well, I can offer you an ethics class for sure, but the New Testament class is by video-conferencing. You'd have a few students in front of you at the Centennial Campus, but students from the other three campuses you would see on three screens."

"I love the New Testament. Could I examine the textbook for the class, to study it?"

Richard considered awhile, then picked a book of the shelf. "Sure," he said. "I'll offer you both Ethics and New Testament for next semester. You can sit in these classes now if you'd like to watch how the other professors instruct. Video-conferencing is not hard once you get the hang of it—there's a technical support person to help you.

"Thank you. I'm thrilled with this opportunity!"

Richard smiled warmly and shook my hand.

For several years I taught Ethics and sometimes New Testament in the fall. In the spring we did missions trips to India and taught in Ywam schools. Both types of classrooms were challenging and fulfilling. At the community college I taught from secular texts, with students from a variety of backgrounds. Christians seemed to love my stories highlighting ethical theories or biblical truths. Other more skeptical students sometimes evaluated me poorly at the end of the semester.

The contrast between classes at PPCC and India was profound. In Lonavala and Bangalore students were hungry for more biblical truth, and eager to apply it on their subsequent two month outreach. Many had come out of Hinduism and were fully persuaded that Jesus was the Son of God—and they wanted more of the Holy Spirit's power in their lives.

Though I continued friendships with a few PPCC students through the years Larry and I especially grew close with the leaders of the Indian schools. We increased financial support as Prabha and Mary—now with two children--began a church planting ministry in the slums. Niebano eventually returned to eastern India and led a large college group at her church. And Vijayan married Luni and took more leadership responsibility at the Bangalore base. We emailed often and prayed for them daily.

I was so grateful to be used in such diverse places, but occasionally I questioned how effective we were. My parents invested decades of their lives to reach the Moni and Dani tribes, so their example often made me wonder, "Where is my tribe?" I called my parents from time to time to talk about this and they prayed with me. Dad reminded me that the Lord has varied callings, and that even Paul had struggled and been misunderstood in his life's work.

One evening in prayer the Lord highlighted a verse from Isaiah 27:6, "He shall cause those who come of Jacob to take root; Israel shall blossom and bud, and fill the face of the world with fruit."

"That's what I'm doing with you and Larry," He told me quietly. "You have discipled and prayed for people all over the world. You are like a plant with branches that has taproots, penetrating far places. You give out my Word, others blossom and bud, and their fruit is the result of your ministry."

I reflected on my years of nursing in Minneapolis, witnessing in Alaska, and caring for people at the Ebro Community Church in northern Minnesota. After marrying Larry there were ten years of discipling single parents, then planting the base in Penang and teaching Asians on mission trips. Then after years of prayer and ministry at New Life Church in Colorado Springs, there were more years teaching in India and Cairo.

"These are your tribe," the Lord reminded me. "They have taken root and filled the face of the world with fruit. Some people are given the gift to minister in one place. Others like Priscilla and Aquilla, Apollos, and Philip minister in numbers of locations. I give each member of my body a different gift and grace. Receive your gift. Embrace it!"

"Thank you, Lord," I whispered. "I'm grateful. Help me to keep seeing this clearly."

Later I recalled three occasions that highlighted the truth God was showing me. First was a time we travelled to Minnesota and Ken and Debbie Peterson hosted a gathering of The Group, the former single parents from Souls Harbor. They were grandparents now, and after pastoring for years Ken was now overseeing the multi campus Union Gospel Mission in St. Paul.

As we sat in a circle in their flowering backyard, Ken turned to us, "We're so grateful for the years you invested in us. I don't know where some of us would be if we hadn't had the fellowship and teaching as single parents." He squeezed Debbie's hand.

"Yes, those were some of my darkest days," Debbie added. "We had each other in the group, and then the Lord put me and Ken together! It's too bad Ken and Patty Freeman couldn't be here now—are they still living in Colorado Springs near you guys, still in Youth with a Mission?"

"Yes," I answered. "So we see them often. But Sharon (Madigan) and Joanne (Holley), we haven't seen you in years. Or Bernita, either. "Hard to believe all of your children have grown up and have kids of their own!"

"Ty and Julie, are you still in the music ministry at Brian and Jacque's church?"

"We are. God has been so good to us and all of our kids," Ty answered. We sat in the large circle reminiscing till dark, and then went inside to worship and pray together.

That weekend we met with others from The Group. We taught at Mark and Shirley Reid's church. Lucy Melena joined us, beaming with joy. She was still an adrenal quickening in the Body who jumpstarted conversations.

The second occasion was a time we visited Colin and Jo White in London on our way back from teaching in Asia. We sat in their living room remembering the 1992 DTS in Penang where they were students. "Do you still keep in close contact with Dass and Rani?" I asked. "I understand you've supported them, and brought them to speak in churches here in England."

"Yes," Jo answered. "And we had a holiday with them at the Red Sea when they led the work in Addis Ababa, Ethiopia. Now they're back in Penang leading the Ywam work, and their children attend Dalat School."

"It's wonderful how your faithful support has helped them carry out their calling," I said.

"Yes, each part of the Body contributes its part so the lost can be reached," Larry added.

"You mean all of my realtor's work counts in the Kingdom," Colin said laughing.

"Yes, and my carpentry work too," Larry smiled.

"And all of your work with the youth here in this part of London!" I added.

The third occasion was a call from a voice I didn't recognize. "This is Mary…Mary Lamb," the voice said. "Do you remember me? I used to babysit Nicky for you when you were married to Zach."

"Mary!" I exclaimed. "Of course I remember you. You were the pretty 12 year old Ojibwe girl with long black hair who was so helpful and kind. How did you get my number?"

"Through Facebook, contacting Zach and then Nick."

"I'm amazed. How are you?"

"I'm doing pretty good, living in Thief River Falls, Minnesota with my sister. I work in accounting at a casino, but I read the Bible and try to get to church sometimes."

"Well, great."

"Years ago when you went through the divorce I felt so badly for you. I've thought about you often, so I decided to try and look you up."

"I'm so glad you did. Do you have children?"

"I have one daughter Toni, but she doesn't live near me. Her dad and I are divorced. I'm planning to move to the Twin Cities and train to be an electrician."

"I'll pray it will work out," I answered. We shared for a long time, and then said goodbye.

"I'll visit you when we next come to Minnesota, Mary. I'm so happy we could connect again. I'll call you next time and we can keep in touch."

"Thanks," Mary replied. "Keep praying for me."

My tribe, amazingly, was found all over the world, wherever the Lord planted me. As Larry and I reached out to others in love they were in turn strengthened to reach out in their worlds. That's the way the gospel can take root and fill the face of the world with fruit. Till every tribe hears.

And Jesus comes.

Amen.

ENDNOTE

McCluskey, Karen Curnow, Editor. *Notes from a Travelling Childhood. Wash. D.C.: Foreign*

Service Youth Foundation, 1994 (Taken from a chapter in this book written by Nina Killham. Chapter is titled WORLD-WISE KIDS (Special Qualities Mark These Global Nomads) (Reprinted with permission from the Feb.17,1990 issue of The Washington Post.)

Marti Anderson is available for speaking engagements and public appearances. For more information contact:

Marti Anderson, D.Min
C/O Advantage Books
P.O. Box 160847
Altamonte Springs, FL 32716

info@findingmytribe.org

To purchase additional copies of this book visit findingmytribe.org

or visit our bookstore website at:
www.advbookstore.com

Longwood, Florida, USA
"we bring dreams to life"™
www.advbookstore.com